What Does It Mean to Be Catholic?

Jane E. Regan • Mimi McReavy Bitzan

Engaging Adults in Meaningful Conversation

LOYOLAPRESS.

CHICAGO

Finding **God**

Our response to God's gifts

Nihil Obstat
Reverend John G. Lodge, S.S.L., S.T.D.
Censor Deputatus
May 18, 2004

Imprimatur
Most Reverend Edwin M. Conway, D.D.
Vicar General
Archdiocese of Chicago
May 24, 2004

The *Nihil Obstat* and *Imprimatur* are official declarations that a book is free of doctrinal and moral error. No implication is contained therein that those who have granted the *Nihil Obstat* and *Imprimatur* agree with the content, opinions, or statements expressed. Nor do they assume any legal responsibility associated with publication.

Cover and Interior Design: Think Design Group

ISBN:0-8294-1903-9
© 2005 Loyola Press. All rights reserved. Manufactured in the United States of America.

LoyolaPress.
3441 N. Ashland Avenue
Chicago, Illinois
(800) 621-1008
FindingGod.org

Printed in [country]
    06 07 08 09 10 ???? 10 9 8 7 6 5 4 3 2

Contents

Introduction

The leadership within our parishes and in the wider Church is recognizing anew the importance of the ongoing faith formation of all members of our faith communities. While attention to the formation of children and youth continues to be of central importance to the life of the Church, there is a growing commitment to set the formation of adults at the center of the work of catechesis.

Both the life of the Church and the dynamics of culture contribute to this growing need for attention to the faith formation of adults. Some examples:

◆ Bookstores are filled with books on "spirituality," many with no apparent link to a particular tradition, designed to address the hunger that many people have for naming what is of real importance to them.
◆ Book clubs and discussion groups continue to appear in a variety of settings across the country in response to people's desire for community and for serious conversation.
◆ The growing awareness of pluralism in this country, particularly religious pluralism, has challenged all of us to examine our own religious identity and to come to some understanding of the religious perspective of others.
◆ Events and trends in the Church have reminded us of the responsibilities we have as adult Christians to be actively involved in the life of the parish and in the leadership of our faith communities.
◆ All of these items contribute to parents' growing awareness of the role they play in the faith life of their children.

These Gathering Sessions give you the resources to provide effective and exciting adult catechesis for the parents of the children in your programs and for all the adults of your parish.

Faith Formation of Adults: An Essential Component

One of the distinguishing characteristics of *Finding God: Our Response to God's Gifts* is the central place adult faith formation holds in the program as a whole. It is an integral part of the program and is woven into the material at every level.

For the Catechists

♦ For each session, catechists are invited to begin their preparation with a "3-Minute Retreat" to set the entire process in the context of prayer.
♦ At the opening of each session, the "Catechist Preparation" pages include background material that is designed to enhance the faith understanding of the catechists.

For the Parents

♦ Each session in the children's books concludes with a parent page: "Raising Faith-Filled Kids." In addition to providing insight into the focus of the session, this page includes suggestions for ways the parents can support their children in connecting their lives with the session's theme.
♦ A parent newsletter (five per year) offers adults inspiration and motivation for recognizing the presence of God in their lives and particularly in their families.

For the Pastor

The Pastor Guide provides the pastor with an overview of *Finding God: Our Response to God's Gifts* and ways to integrate the program into the wider parish community.

For All Adults

Beyond their roles as catechists, parents, or pastor, the adults of the parish are invited to come together for meaningful conversation in the Gathering Sessions.

> *Every theme covered by formation should feed, in the first place, the faith of the catechist. It is true that catechists catechize others by firstly catechizing themselves.*
>
> GDC 239

Religious Educator as Leader of Faith

We know that the faith formation of our catechists is essential to the life of our program and to the effective catechesis of our adults, youth, and children. Your own ongoing faith formation as a catechetical leader is equally important to the effectiveness and vitality of your parish or school religious education program. That's clear in the Director Guide, where you'll find invitations to prayer and reflection designed especially for you.

Within the preparation for each of the Gathering Sessions in this book are an overview of the session's theme and an invitation to take your own time for prayer and reflection. Designed to be used within the process of preparing for the Gathering Session, the "Leader's 3-Minute Retreat" provides

◆ an opportunity to reflect on the core scripture used during the session and

◆ an invitation to name your own response to God's invitation heard in the session.

We encourage you to give yourself time for these "3-Minute Retreats." If you are working with a team of people, these are perfect to use as the opening of the planning time for each session.

The five Gathering Sessions are described on the following pages.

Overview of the Gathering Sessions

What Does It Mean to Be Catholic?

Session A
God's Invitation and Our Response

At the heart of our understanding of God is the dynamic interaction of God's invitation and our response. This invitation is spoken most clearly in Jesus Christ—it is in Jesus that we get a sense of the depth of relationship to which God is calling us. Our response to this invitation is faith and an openness to participate in the many ways God's presence is made known to us.

This session examines the dynamic at the heart of our relationship with God, that of invitation-response. Participants discuss the ways in which they are aware of God's presence in their lives and the way our Catholic faith supports us in our response to God.

Session B
"Who Do You Say That I Am?"

"Who do you say that I am?" Two thousand years ago, Jesus asked this question of his disciples and followers. Jesus asks this same question of us today: "Who do you say that I am?" This is the fundamental Christian question because in naming who Jesus is, we gain insight into who we are and how we live our lives.

This session highlights the different ways the Gospel writers portrayed Jesus as they attempted to respond to the questions and experiences of their day. The session examines Gospel images of Jesus with particular focus on Jesus as Teacher, Healer, Friend, and Savior. Participants reflect on their images of Jesus and the meanings these images have for the way they live.

Session C
Living the Catholic Tradition

Why am I a Catholic? Different people have different responses. While these differences in perspective can lead to tension within the Church, there is good news within our Catholic tradition—both a respect for the past and an eye on the future are key elements in what it means to live our lives as Catholics.

This session allows adults to reflect on their understanding of the Church as a living tradition and recognize the way the Church builds on the past (memory) while being aware of and responding to the contemporary world (openness). Participants examine their sense of the balance of memory and openness and its expression in their parish.

Session D
Invitation to the Feast

The Eucharist is "the sum and summary of our faith." (*CCC* 1327) The Eucharist serves as a context within which to recommit ourselves to recognizing the body of Christ—present under the forms of bread and wine and present within the community of faith.

This session allows adults to reflect on their understanding of liturgy with a particular focus on the Eucharist. The session highlights the way the Eucharist reflects the invitation-response dynamic that is at the heart of Catholic theology and discusses ways in which the participants can more fully experience Sunday liturgy.

Session E
Let Your Conscience Be Your Guide

The same invitation-response dynamic examined throughout this year's themes comes into play here. We respond to God's gift of grace by living lives marked by love and justice.

This session allows adults to reflect on the role of conscience in moral decision making. The session highlights factors that contribute to the development of a well-formed conscience, as well as the resources Catholics can use to help make good moral decisions.

List of Abbreviations

CCC — *Catechism of the Catholic Church*

CSL — Constitution on the Sacred Liturgy

GCD — General Catechetical Directory

GDC — *General Directory for Catechesis*

OHWB — *Our Hearts Were Burning Within Us*

Adult Faith Formation

The call for adult faith formation has been an explicit part of Church documents on religious education since the end of the 1960s. The General Catechetical Directory that was published in 1971 includes the often quoted line cited here. And yet most of us involved in catechesis are aware of the challenges of planning and implementing effective adult religious education experiences.

At the same time, we recognize—and many of us have experienced—the powerful transformative results when adults in our parishes are energized by their faith and committed to bringing their faith into everyday life. So how do we go about bringing into line our convictions about the necessity of adult faith formation and the promise that it holds with the realities of parish life?

Shifts to Adult Faith Formation

An important starting point is to name that making the catechesis of adults the "chief form of catechesis" (*GDC* 59) involves significant shifts in the way that we often think about religious education. Three of them are key.

1. From Information to Transformation

We certainly recognize that many adults would profit from learning more information about Church teachings and practices. But the information is not enough. It is not information for its own sake, but information that is in service of formation and transformation that is a sign of genuine adult catechesis.

Catechesis for adults, since it deals with persons who are capable of an adherence that is fully responsible, must be considered the chief form of catechesis. All the other forms, which are indeed always necessary, are in some way oriented to it.

GCD 20

A discussion of these shifts can be found in an article by Jane Regan, "Adult Faith Formation: Will It Catch on This Time?" (America September 22, 2003, pages 18–21)

By the way we structure adult faith formation, we can invite adults to look beyond the "what" of our tradition to the "so what?" So what difference does this make to how I live my life, raise my children, spend my money, and engage in the political dynamics of my town and state?

2. From Programs to Process

The call for a new focus on adult faith formation is often interpreted as a call for more programs, more lectures, or more Lenten series. However, if we are seeing adult faith formation as not exclusively about information but in service to transformation, then the best process is not lecture but conversation. The most effective programs are those that provide a process for adults to explore the tradition in a way that allows for sustained, critical conversation.

3. From Membership to Mission

When we look at our parishes, we recognize a variety of contexts in which groups of adults gather for instruction and formation—the catechists, the lectors, the RCIA team, and many more. Each of these gatherings serves as an opportunity for participants to deepen their sense of commitment to the parish and to gain further insight into their particular ministry.

But the goal of adult faith formation is not only to enhance the faith life of the participant and strengthen the parish. Adult faith formation invites the believing community to look beyond their own community to the wider mission of the Church.

Over the next few pages, we outline the ways in which the Gathering Sessions, in both content and format, help you to achieve these key shifts in your own parish.

Goals of Adult Faith Formation: Toward Transformation

As we said earlier, adult catechesis is about more than information alone. It is about information as it is in service to formation and transformation. But *what* transformation? What aspects of human life are addressed in this process of transformation?

In exploring the nature of adult catechesis, the writers of *Our Hearts Were Burning Within Us* name three goals that direct and broaden the work of adult faith formation. When we think about the work of adult catechesis, we need to attend to each of these three goals. It is important that the vision of any formation we do with adults keeps each of these elements in balance.

> *In response to God's call to holiness, our faith and life as adult disciples are grounded in developing a personal relationship with Jesus, "the Holy One of God" (Jn 6:69, Mk 1:24).*
>
> OHWB, 68

1. Invite and enable ongoing conversion to Jesus in holiness of life

At the core of all catechesis is the task of fostering an ever closer relationship with Jesus Christ. The *General Directory for Catechesis* refers to this as apprenticeship—a shaping of one's life and actions so as to reflect the call to holiness.

The process that shapes the Gathering Sessions continually invites participants to engage in experiences and conversations that encourage conversion—a realigning of their lives in light of their relationship with Christ. Thus, prayer, guided meditation, and reflection serve as important elements of this program as they provide opportunities that invite participants to experience conversion.

2. Promote and support active membership in the Catholic community

In addition to inviting adults in your parish to deepen their relationship with Jesus Christ, participants in the Gathering Sessions are also given the opportunity to reaffirm their membership within the Church and their connection with their particular parish. For some adults, participating in the Gathering Sessions may well be the beginning of a new level of engagement with the parish.

Establishing an atmosphere of hospitality and welcome is often the first step in inviting adults into active membership in the Church. Essential elements in addressing this goal include

- scheduling time for socializing before and after each Gathering Session,
- providing accurate information about other parish activities,
- integrating the Gathering Sessions with the children's program, with programing for the rest of the faith community, and particularly with the liturgical life of the parish.

3. Call and prepare adults to act as disciples in the world
The fundamental link between catechesis and evangelization is at the heart of this goal. A renewed understanding of evangelization has developed in the years following the Second Vatican Council.

Evangelization, simply stated, is the proclamation of the reality of God's presence in human history, a proclamation in both word and action. Catechesis in all of its forms, but particularly with adults, has as a primary goal the transformation of a parish into an evangelizing community—a Church where adults take seriously their task of being sent out as disciples in service to the world.

Integrated into the Gathering Sessions are opportunities for the participants to look beyond their own lives and beyond the parish community and to recognize their role as disciples. These opportunities include the questions that are given to guide small-group conversation, the invitations to prayer and reflection, and the many ways in which people are invited to respond to God's invitations in a way that reflects God's presence in the world.

The Church and its adult faithful have a mission in and to the world: to share the message of Christ to renew and to transform the social and temporal order. This dual calling to evangelization and justice is integral to the identity of the lay faithful; all are called to it in baptism.

OHWB, 72

The Heart of Adult Catechesis: Conversation

If the goals of adult catechesis set information at the service of transformation, pride of place goes to a process rooted in conversation. Not just simple chatting, but sustained, critical conversation. Conversation is "sustained" in that it takes place regularly over an extended period of time, and each conversation is long enough to allow for a genuine interchange of experience, insights, and commitments. It is "critical" in that the conversation is guided in a manner that invites participants to examine and articulate not only their beliefs and experiences of faith but also the source of those beliefs and their implications for living the Christian life.

The design of the Gathering Sessions places emphasis on the centrality of the process of conversation to adult faith formation. At each point of the catechetical process, attention is given to addressing the theme in a way that invites participants to bring their own lives and experience into the event. In a more structured way, the Explore part of each Gathering Session consists of two parts—the first is the presentation of the session's theme, and the second is an opportunity for small-group conversation and response.

At the most fundamental level, the very concept of the Gathering Sessions is to create a *space* where conversation can be freely engaged.

- The first is the physical space. Attention to comfort, aesthetics, and details are all in service of creating a space where adults can gather to talk with other adults about things that matter.
- In addition to the physical space, there is the space that is shaped by hospitality. It is to be a safe space where the telling of stories is welcome and the recalling of faith experiences is heard as just that—a person's experience.
- And finally, there needs to be temporal space, that is, the Gathering Sessions provide time for the sustained, critical conversation that marks effective adult faith formation.

> *Evangelizing is in fact the grace and vocation proper to the Church, her deepest identity. She exists in order to evangelize . . .*
>
> *Apostolic Exhortation on Evangelization, 14*

The Promise of Adult Catechesis: An Evangelizing Church

A renewed understanding of evangelization has developed in the years following the Second Vatican Council. In the past evangelization might have been seen as the work of the few in proclaiming the Good News in lands where the Gospel had not yet been heard. Now, however, a renewed focus on evangelization places it at the very center of the life of the Church. As proclaimed in the *Apostolic Exhortation on Evangelization* in 1975 and echoed in several documents since then, the Church exists in order to evangelize. That is the Church's reason for being.

The renewed call to attend with care and diligence to the Church's mission of evangelization is a strong mandate and clear rationale for the work of adult faith formation. The goal of adult faith formation is not only to enhance the faith life of the participant and strengthen the parish community. It does these things in order to respond better to the Church's primary task and reason for being—to evangelize. The *General Directory for Catechesis* is clear on this: Adult catechesis has as a central goal forming, strengthening, and challenging the adult faith community to be active participants in this task.

This responsibility to evangelize is both corporate and individual. The Church and the members that make it up have the role of both announcing the reign of God and contributing to its realization. Catechesis in all of its forms, but particularly with adults, has as a primary goal the formation of an evangelizing community—a Church that takes seriously its task of being sent out as disciples in service to the world.

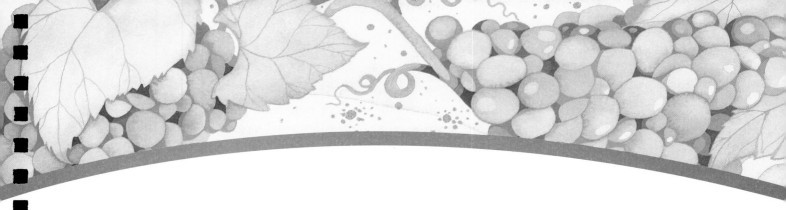

Using the Catechetical Model

The catechetical model that is used in each Gathering Session corresponds with the model that is used in the rest of *Finding God: Our Response to God's Gifts.*

The Director Guide (pages 56–62) provides a detailed discussion of the catechetical model. We pause here just to remember that the foundation of the model is rooted in Ignatian spirituality.

Fundamental to this is the recognition that all that we have and are originates and flows from God's love for us. In a most radical way, all of the Christian life can be understood as response to God's invitation of love. The only adequate response to this invitation is faith.

As a whole, the movement of each Gathering Session evokes this dynamic of invitation and response across four basic steps.

◆ **Engage**—We gather our thoughts and ideas around a theme that is a point of entry into our Catholic tradition and to our awareness of God's presence in our lives.

◆ **Explore**—In the Scriptures and Tradition, we hear God's invitation to relationship and to an apprenticeship to Jesus. And we hear that same invitation in the day-to-day experience of people in our faith community.

◆ **Reflect**—Our response to this invitation is first prayer—prayer of gratitude for God's invitation, prayer for increased awareness of God's presence in our lives, in the lives of those around us, and in the world.

◆ **Respond**—And our response is to ask, "So what?" So, what does this mean for my life? for my relationship with my family? for how I make decisions at work, at home, with my friends?

A discussion of each of the four movements as they are expressed in the Gathering Sessions gives you a sense of the look and feel of the Sessions. The time frame here is based on 60 minutes (plus time for refreshments). Ideas for adapting the model for longer periods can be found on page 30.

Welcome

While not a formal part of the catechetical model that shapes the Gathering Session, it is nonetheless an important component of the time you are sharing with the adults in your parish. Providing a welcoming and hospitable space isn't simply a "nice touch." It is a way we extend the invitation and love of God to one another.

Keep in Mind

◆ Be present to the participants as they come in; welcome them as you would if they were coming into your home.
◆ Remember that for some parents/adults in your parish, their children's participation in faith formation and these Gathering Sessions are the only connection they have with the parish.
◆ Let the participants know that you are prepared for them and awaiting their arrival by having everything that is needed set out in advance—handouts, name tags, pens or pencils, and so forth.
◆ Be sure to have other members of the parish staff or facilitators around to welcome and greet the participants.

Engage

Through reflection, the comments of others, or conversation with those sitting near us, we are invited to recognize the connection between the session's theme and our day-to-day lives. Prayer is always a part of this movement—prayers acknowledging God's presence as we gather to grow in our faith.

Keep in Mind

◆ Beginning with energy, enthusiasm, and words of welcome is key.
◆ As the session moves into a time of prayer, *don't rush.* Times of prayer include silence as well as song, reflection as well as readings.

Explore

The presentation breaks open the theme and explores the teachings and traditions of the Church. The stories told and the concepts examined within the presentation help lead into small-group conversation that provides an opportunity for participants to explore how the message of the session affects the way they understand their faith and the way they live their lives. The time for conversation provides the opportunity for the adults to "go deeper" into the topic of the Gathering Session.

Keep in Mind

◆ Prepare the presentation to best fit your own style. In the sessions in this guide, the left column contains an outline of the presentation, and the right column is the "script."

◆ Each presentation includes a "dramatic" piece that can be read by one or more participants. For your convenience, participant readings appear in blue type within the session text. Be sure to pick people who have a flair for the dramatic!

◆ Keep the presentation to about 20 minutes. This allows for conversation time, even in the setting where you only have an hour.

◆ The carefully worded questions that are included in the session handouts serve to guide the conversation.

◆ Each small group includes a facilitator who serves as host for the conversation. His or her role is to introduce the questions, keep the conversation flowing, and invite everyone to participate.

◆ Small groups can be formed in many different ways. Group numbers or colored dots on name tags work well for larger groups. For smaller groups, it works to simply "count off" into groups of six or seven (including facilitators).

◆ Following the small-group conversation and once the full group is regathered, invite comments or insights from the small groups. Ask the facilitators to be ready to make a brief observation on their groups' conversation.

Reflect

We are invited to respond to the invitation of God's love present in the session's theme. We begin by quieting our surroundings and ourselves; this allows us to become aware of God's presence and to be quiet in that awareness. Time for quiet reflection leads to a communal expression of gratitude to God as well as prayers that we might respond to God's invitation with faith.

Keep in Mind

- As we invite the participants into time of quiet reflection, prepare the atmosphere by playing soft music.
- Take your time as you read the opening reflection; be aware of your own breathing as a way of pacing the phrases.

Respond

We respond to God's gifts through prayer and through lives that are reflective of the Gospel. To conclude the Gathering Session we consider ways to grow in our understanding of the key concepts presented at the gathering and to share our faith with our families.

Keep in Mind

- Bring energy and enthusiasm even to this last part of the session.
- In addition to highlighting sections of the handout, be sure to mention parish events that could be of interest.
- If there are a lot of other announcements, think about preparing an additional handout rather than making this section unduly long.

Refreshments

It is important that our time together begin and end with a sense of hospitality. Having some light refreshments available is a good way to end the Gathering Session. It encourages people to stay around and continue the conversation.

Keep in Mind

- Keep things simple, small, and easy to eat.
- Have someone responsible for keeping the trays filled and the juice and coffee flowing.
- Don't forget napkins and a wastebasket!

Toward a Successful Program

In addition to understanding the importance of adult learning and the theories of how adults learn and grow in faith, it is essential that those who direct faith formation programs for adults also keep in mind practical considerations to help insure success. The following guidelines offer tips for implementing effective faith formation opportunities for adults. Read on, share the guidelines with members of your parish staff, and add your own insights and tips along the way.

Top Ten Guidelines for Effective Adult Faith Formation: What To Do

1. The most important question must always be, "So what?" Provide time during each Gathering Session for critical reflection. It is very important for adults to ask, "So what?" So . . . what difference does this teaching of the Church or this message of the Gospel make to the way I live my life?

   ◆ Take time at your gatherings to listen to people. Often, the time before the gathering starts and after it ends provides excellent opportunities for really connecting with people.

   ◆ Make sure the questions for small-group discussion are interesting and direct.

2. Lose the lecture.

Too many times, those who plan adult faith formation sessions simply bring in a speaker to present a topic. We need to do much better than this! Adults learn and grow in faith through a wide variety of experiences.

◆ Incorporate prayer, quiet reflection, guided imagery, conversation, service, music, stories, and drama in your faith formation programs for adults.

◆ If you do bring in a speaker, make sure the speaker's presentation includes real-life stories that help illustrate key points.

◆ Prepare speakers by telling them important things to know or understand about your parish and your parishioners.

3. Make a commitment.

It won't happen by magic. You have to pay for good adult faith formation programs. If your parish believes that adult faith formation is important and says that lifelong learning is a priority, then the parish budget and resources need to reflect this.

◆ Know what resources your parish now uses to support your adult faith formation programs. Include financial resources, paid staff time, and volunteer hours.

◆ If needed, make plans with the pastoral staff and pastoral council to begin to reallocate resources toward adult faith formation opportunities. If you can't take a giant leap in this direction, at least take small steps.

4. Faith formation is a team sport.

If you want to convey the importance of adult learning, then the entire pastoral team needs to be on deck— planning, evaluating, and leading.

◆ Find ways for each member of the parish staff to contribute and participate in adult faith formation gatherings.

◆ If you don't have a large staff, find ways to involve members of the pastoral council or religious education committee.

5. Language: Get Real.
   Use language that helps people connect faith and the teachings of the Church with the way they live their lives.

   - Avoid "churchy" language in presentations and written materials. For example, when speaking with adults in your parish, you can be sure that a word like *hermeneutical* is not helpful.
   - Resources such as *U.S. Catholic* magazine can provide ideas of how to use real-life language and stories to explore theological concepts and church teaching.

6. Connect with the Church's liturgical year.
   When scheduling programs for adults, pay close attention to the liturgical seasons as an important dimension of parish life and a source of direction for planning.

   - Find ways to connect the prayer experiences of a gathering with the liturgical year. Use an Advent wreath during Advent, for example, or the color purple during Lent.
   - When possible, incorporate hymns, songs, and Scripture from a recent Sunday Liturgy into the adult gathering.
   - Look to Lent as an opportune time to offer a mini-series on a faith-related topic for adults or a special retreat.

7. Creativity is essential.
   Find ways to engage the imaginations of the adults. Don't just *talk* about the message, let adults *experience* it through art, music, drama, reflection, and shared conversation.

   - Don't be afraid to include wonderful children's stories, guided reflections, or retreat experiences that have been successful with youth in prayer experiences for adults.
   - Find ways to make good music a part of adult faith formation experiences.

8. Dessert is not optional.

Create an atmosphere of welcome and hospitality. Treat your participants as honored guests. Serve food (good food).

- If your Gathering Session is in the morning, serving coffee and tea prior to and, where possible, during the session is important.
- Having even the simplest dessert set out on trays adds to the feeling of hospitality. Be sure to have a selection of items for those with allergies or staying away from sweets. You might have cut-up fruits and vegetables, cheese, and crackers.
- Have someone responsible for making sure that everyone is served.

9. Timing is everything.

Make a schedule and stick to it. If you start on time and end on time, you'll gain a great deal of respect and you'll keep people coming back.

- Ask others (facilitators or parish staff) to help you keep to the schedule.
- Take time to evaluate the flow and timing of an event and learn from it. Make adjustments as needed and you will continue to improve and enhance future gatherings.

10. Have fun!

Weave humor and good fun into the flow of the Gathering Session. Go out of your way to spice up your times together and make them fun.

- Special touches like flowers on a table or lighted candles can go a long way to creating an environment that reflects welcome.
- Award a door prize at the end of a gathering to one of your guests. Prizes might be a candle, a book, or a free ticket to a parish breakfast.

Top Ten Pitfalls for Adult Faith Formation: What *Not* To Do

Whether you are an experienced pro or new to the enterprise of adult faith formation, it is important to avoid some key pitfalls that can sabotage a potentially successful program. Here are some important ones to keep in mind.

1. Lack of hospitality

Much more than the presentation you give or the handouts you create, the way you welcome adult participants is your greatest opportunity for evangelization. Don't miss it! When you welcome adults to a faith formation program, keep in mind that going to Mass on Sunday and participating in parish life may not be a regular part of their lives. Don't miss this opportunity to welcome people back with open arms!

So, when you gather with adults, do the following:
- Have greeters at the doors.
- Light the candles, put out the flowers, play your best music, and serve delicious food.
- Ask staff and facilitators to serve as hosts.
- Mingle with your guests. Talk with them. Listen to their stories.

2. Fear of commitment

You cannot run a successful program on low provisions. If your parish is making a commitment to adult faith formation, the allocation of parish resources should reflect this commitment.
- **Staff time:** The pastoral team needs time for ongoing study, planning, preparation, and evaluation.
- **Budget:** Be prepared to cover the cost of speakers, resources, handouts, volunteer appreciation, food, and other expenses.
- **Volunteer hours:** When many people put in lots of volunteer hours, the result is widespread ownership and commitment.

3. Repeat, repeat, repeat . . .

If you repeat the same program year after year without evaluating or making changes, it is very likely that your program will soon become stale and out of touch with people's lives.
- Take time to evaluate each adult faith formation gathering. Keep notes to help you make improvements throughout the year.

- At the end of the year, invest a substantial amount of time in evaluating the overall effectiveness of the past year's events.
- Seek out the ideas, input, and comments of the adults who participated in this year's programs to improve and enhance programs for next year.
- As you move through a year, pay close attention to the specific needs, interests, and concerns of the group with whom you are working. These will change from year to year, and a successful program will reflect this.

4. The Lone Ranger approach

One person cannot run a successful program by himself or herself. Planning and implementing successful and effective faith formation programs for adults requires a great team of people.

- Involve members of the parish staff, members of the parish faith formation (religious education) committee, people on the facilitator team, or Catholic school faculty and staff in planning and evaluating faith formation opportunities for adults.
- Find ways for the various groups within the parish (musicians, speakers, catechists, facilitators) to give their best talent and creativity to create and implement the Gathering Sessions.

5. Missing the wisdom of the community

Beware of speakers who tell you they must have an hour or longer because they simply cannot cover all that the participants need to know in a shorter time. This kind of attitude shows a lack of appreciation for the wisdom of the listeners.

- Select and invite speakers who explore Church tradition and teaching and tell stories of faith in ways that evoke stories of faith from the participants.
- Spend time with those who will be giving the presentation to be sure that they understand the focus of the year and the role that they serve.

6. Failure to flow

Each element of a gathering is important, and it is essential to give time and attention to creating and developing each piece. You give power to what you pay attention to. To be really effective, be sure that each element of a gathering flows into the next.

- Keep the time for prayer and reflection, presentation, and conversation in balance.
- Remember that it takes time to shift from one activity to the next and factor that in to your Gathering Session schedule.
- Be sure to begin on time and end on time.

7. Skipping the discussion time

In the Gathering Sessions, the conversation is given the same amount of time as the presentation. It is when adults talk with other adults about the significance of the faith for their lives that real growth in faith happens.

- Pay attention to time. If you start late, the discussion is usually where time is made up.
- Make clear in the way you introduce the conversation time that you understand this part of the session to be of key importance.
- Be sure that the groups are small enough for genuine conversation. Usually six or seven is a good number.

8. Dismissing the details

When you plan a gathering with adults, know that the details are important.

- Take time to rehearse parts of the gathering that require special preparation.
- Practice your welcoming statements out loud and in front of a microphone. Write out transitions from one part of the session to the next so that your directions are clear and concise.
- Before the meeting begins, make sure the sound system works and that your handouts are ready.
- Take time to think about how you will conclude your meeting. Be sure that your gathering ends with good energy and lets the guests know that you and the rest of the parish staff were delighted to have had this time with them.

9. Volunteer Void

Most of your volunteers are accustomed to working with children or youth, not with adults.

- Provide ongoing training and support to help your volunteers (facilitators) learn how to respond to the needs of adults.
- Find creative ways to support your volunteers with affirmation and appreciation. Give thanks and keep giving thanks.
- Throw a great party at the end of the year!

10. And another thing!

One member of the parish staff wants to offer Lenten Bible studies, an involved parishioner thinks that starting up a soup kitchen is the direction to go. Too often, there is a tendency in parishes to add program after program for adults without thinking about what you really want or where you are headed. Be clear about your vision for adult faith formation in your parish, and communicate this vision to others.

Making It Work

The Gathering Sessions are an essential component of *Finding God: Our Response to God's Gifts.* These sessions for adults, along with the other elements of the program, work together to form a total parish faith formation experience. Gathering Sessions, like other elements of adult faith formation, are most effective when they are part of an overall pastoral plan of the parish and when they fit into the present rhythm and schedule of parish life.

Fitting into the Pastoral Plan of the Parish

Begin the process of integrating the Gathering Sessions into the life of your parish by recognizing the structures of faith formation that are already present: the catechetical program for children and youth, the youth ministry program, and sacramental formation. Perhaps there are already in place Bible studies, prayer groups, or small faith-sharing groups. Naming (and affirming) these opportunities is essential to shaping a total parish faith formation experience.

The Gathering Sessions, since they work thematically with *Finding God: Our Response to God's Gifts*, can serve as a point of unity for the many opportunities for formation, particularly adult formation, that take place in the life of the parish. This season's theme, "What Does It Mean to Be Catholic?" and the way the theme is played out in these five sessions could easily serve as a foundation for extended opening prayer and reflection for the Parish Council. It could be integrated into the movement of the youth group for the year. It might serve as a helpful lens through which to plan a Lenten series or the annual retreat for the older adults in your parish.

In ways that are appropriate for your setting, work to integrate the Gathering Sessions into the rhythm and flow of your parish. Help others to see that this isn't limited to those who have children in the religious education program: this is part of the ongoing faith formation of the entire parish.

Possible Schedules and Formats

The writers of the *General Directory for Catechesis* remind us that a well-coordinated catechetical program enhances the effectiveness of all faith formation.

Schedule

There is no place where that need for coordination is clearer than in the scheduling of activities within a parish. Some suggestions follow.

- If this is one of the parish's first ventures into ongoing adult faith formation, you might find it easier to begin with two or three of the five sessions.
- Keep in mind the liturgical year and the way the Gathering Sessions can complement the rhythm of Church life.
- Also be aware of the schedule of other programs and meetings within the parish. When do key social events happen in your parish? When does the youth group have their fundraising talent show? You will certainly want to avoid the parent-teacher conference evenings.
- Get the schedule set and out to those involved as soon as possible; family calendars fill up quickly!

Format

The time frame given in the Gathering Sessions is based on an hour. This timing is particularly helpful if you are scheduling the adult sessions at the same time as those for the children.

If you have more time, consider the following, being sure to maintain the time balance among the three main aspects of prayer and reflection, presentation, and conversation.

- Add music to the opening prayer (Engage), perhaps a song that is used in the children's program. Or enhance the Reflect section by expanding the opening meditation, allowing more time for silence.
- Weave your own stories or the stories of the parish into the presentation section of Explore.
- Allow more time for full-group conversation after the small groups, having each of the groups report back.
- Simply allow the refreshment time at the end to be more leisurely and relaxed.

The coordination of catechesis is not merely a strategic factor, aimed at more effective evangelization, but has a profound theological meaning. Evangelizing activity must be well coordinated because it touches on the unity of faith, which sustains all the Church's actions.

General Directory for Catechesis, 272

Recruiting and Training Facilitators

One of the most significant aspects of the Gathering Sessions is the role of the facilitators who serve as hosts and facilitate the small-group conversations. These facilitators may be the only parish leaders with whom some families come into contact. They are the front-line evangelists. Giving careful thought to recruiting and training the facilitators is an essential first step to successfully implementing this program.

In compiling your list of possible facilitators,
- look around you before liturgy or afterwards at coffee time and note those who are "regulars" but not already involved in a lot of activities;
- review the names of families with children in the parish program for a parent who might be interested;
- consider asking members of the parish staff, catechists, or members of the Parish Council;
- think of people who are not involved in your parish program because working with children or youth is not one of their gifts—this could be the perfect spot for them.

What are the qualities that make people good facilitators? Good facilitators are people who
- enjoy making others feel welcome,
- are good listeners—who can get others to talk about their experiences and share their stories,
- are open and respectful of different points of view,
- desire to continue to grow in their own faith understanding, and
- have a sense of humor.

How many facilitators will you need? Estimate the number of participants you'll have in each Gathering Session. Usually small-group conversation works best with five to seven people in the group, including the facilitator. You will need one facilitator for each group. Add at least two more for "back-up."

The facilitators' task is to lead the small groups in conversation. A good facilitator both keeps the group on topic and serves as a link between the small group and the group as a whole. This section includes a training workshop for facilitators (pages 35–48). Scheduling this workshop should take place early in the planning process.

Basic Preparation for Every Session

The setup and format for each of the sessions is similar. The items listed below apply to all of the sessions. Check the specific session for particular preparation needs.

To Do Well in Advance of the Gathering Session

☐ Set dates for Gathering Sessions. Try to arrange topics to coordinate with liturgical seasons and parish events.

☐ Invite parish staff to help host the sessions. Determine the role each will play.

☐ In addition to those expected to attend, ask parish staff to identify different "target groups" to invite to each session. (See suggestions listed with each session.)

☐ Recruit a team of facilitators to help host and facilitate small-group conversation.

To Do Two Weeks Beforehand

☐ Submit bulletin announcements. (See pages 33–34.)

☐ Send letters of invitation to members of target groups.

☐ Send home reminders with children in the parish faith formation program, sacramental programs, and/or school.

☐ Confirm the presence and participation of enough trained facilitators. You may wish to send them copies of the four page session handout to help them prepare.

☐ Reserve the space you need and plan for such requirements as welcome table, podium, sound system, seating, space for small-group conversation, table for refreshments.

☐ Arrange for volunteers to help with welcome, refreshments, and clean up.

☐ Carefully read through the entire session noting the need for readers for Scripture and various "dramatic" pieces. Ask participants to do the various readings and get copies to them in advance of the session.

☐ Make arrangements for music to enhance prayer and quiet reflection (musicians or CD players).

☐ Add your own notes to personalize the introduction and presentation.

☐ Prepare the presentation. Check timing and make adjustments as necessary.

For the Gathering Session

☐ Duplicate the necessary handouts.

☐ Set out copies of the readings and carefully mark Scripture passages in a Bible.

☐ Prepare the welcome table with nametags, markers, handouts, paper, pens, wastebaskets. Add flowers if you like and a CD player to have music playing as guests arrive. You may want to set out information on other parish programs.

☐ Complete setup for the presentation, conversation, and refreshments. Check to make sure everything is ready and greeters are in place before guests arrive.

☐ Have a plan in place for receiving feedback on the session.

Sample Bulletin Announcements

For Gathering Session A
Gods Invitation and Our Response

Insert day, date, time, place
From the time of the patriarchs and the prophets until this very moment—God is continually inviting each of us to deepen our relationship with Him and with one another. But when was the last time we really listened to God's invitation? When was the last time we were truly aware of God's presence and love around us?

Join us for this important Gathering Session as we come together to explore the meaning of God's invitation in our lives. How will we respond? For more information, contact:

For Gathering Session B
"Who Do You Say That I Am?"

Insert day, date, time, place
"Who do you say that I am?" Two thousand years ago, Jesus asked his followers this question. Jesus asks this same question of us today: "Who do you say that I am?"

Join us for this Gathering Session as we deepen our understanding of Jesus as Teacher, Healer, Friend, and Savior. As faithful disciples of Jesus, we need to live as Jesus lived and love as Jesus loved. For more information, contact:

For Gathering Session C
Living the Catholic Tradition

Insert day, date, time, place
Why am I Catholic? Different people will have different responses. Some may say they like the traditions of the Church that provide a steady presence in a changing world. Other people will say that they like the way the Church is open to dealing with changing times and needs. Respect for the past *and* openness to change—*both* are important parts of being Catholic today.

Join us for this Gathering Session as we explore the reasons we have for being Catholic and the difference our Catholic faith makes in the way we choose to live our lives. For more information, contact:

For Gathering Session D
Invitation to the Feast

Insert day, date, time, place
Why do we get up and go to Mass? For some of us, going to Mass on Sunday has become an obligation—something we try to squeeze into an already busy weekend, or something we just don't get to because life gets too hectic.

Join us for this Gathering Session as we come together to examine ways to make going to Mass on Sunday more meaningful for us as adults and for our families. For more information, contact:

For Gathering Session E
Let Your Conscience Be Your Guide

Insert day, date, time, place
Throughout our lives, we're faced with making countless decisions. Many of these decisions we make quickly, without really giving them a second thought. But some decisions can be harder to make. Sometimes a decision can leave us feeling confused or unsure of what we should do.

Join us for this special Gathering Session as we look at how we make good moral decisions in our lives. We'll explore the steps we can we take and resources we can use. For more information, contact:

Facilitator Workshop

The people who serve as facilitators of small-group conversations play a key role in the successful implementation of the faith formation experiences offered in this program. In each of the Gathering Sessions, small-group conversation provides opportunities for adult participants to connect the message of the Gospel and teachings of the Church with their own faith and life experiences. Facilitators help participants make these connections. In addition to leading small-group discussions, facilitators help host the Gathering Sessions by fostering a spirit of hospitality and welcome.

Leader's 3-Minute Retreat

As you prepare for this training session with the facilitators for this program, take some time for your own reflection on the role of a leader in faith formation and people in your life who have helped you grow in your faith.

For Your Reflection

Reflect on your own personal journey of faith and think about the people who have been important to you along the way. Who has had an impact on you? Who has been a sign of Christ's presence for you? What have you learned from them? Take a moment now to give thanks to God for the gift of these people in your life.

> Let the word of Christ dwell in you richly, as in all wisdom you teach and admonish one another, singing psalms, hymns, and spiritual songs with gratitude in your hearts to God. And whatever you do, in word or in deed, do everything in the name of the Lord Jesus, giving thanks to God the Father through him.
>
> Col. 3:16–17

Overview and Agenda

Central Theme

Adults learn best when they are given the opportunity to be in conversation with one another about matters of faith. The facilitator's role is to help make this happen.

Objectives

In this session, persons who have volunteered to serve as facilitators will

* build and strengthen a sense of community among themselves by getting to know one another.

* explore the role facilitators play in helping create an atmosphere of hospitality and welcome at the Gathering Sessions.

* deepen their understanding of the importance of small-group conversation in adult faith formation and explore ways to effectively facilitate and guide small-group discussions.

Schedule

10 minutes	Welcome and Opening Prayer
20 minutes	Presentation
20 minutes	Small-Group Conversation
15 minutes	Feedback from the groups/ Discussion of small-group scenarios
10 minutes	Announcements and Closing Prayer
15 minutes	Refreshments

To Do Before the Facilitator Workshop

☐ Notify the facilitators about this training session well in advance.

☐ Invite members of the parish staff to participate in the session.

☐ Ask volunteers to assist you in implementing the session. You will need greeters, people to host the name-tag table and distribute handouts, and a reader. You may wish to recruit people to help with serving refreshments and some to assist with clean up afterwards.

Setup

This session requires a space for Opening Prayer and Presentation and space for the participants to move into small groups following the presentation. Set up a microphone/sound system if necessary.

Presentation: Consider setting the chairs in a U shape so participants can see one another. Place a low table in the center with a Bible, candle, plant, and cloth.

Small-group conversation: Have small circles of chairs set up behind the participants for small-group conversations, or ask the participants to take their chairs and move into small groups themselves after the presentation.

Refreshments: Set up a place for participants to enjoy a beverage and/or snack following the session.

In addition, have the following available:

☐ Welcome table with a name tag for each participant. Have additional name tags, markers, and wastebaskets available.

☐ A Bible with Colossians 3:11–17 clearly marked.

☐ Copies of the Facilitator Workshop handout for participants and paper and pens for facilitators to record responses and questions during small-group conversation.

WELCOME

Welcome, everyone!

(Leader introduces himself or herself and other members of the parish staff who are present.)

The role of facilitator is to welcome participants and guide conversation.

Thank you for being with us. Thanks for agreeing to serve as facilitators for this year's Gathering Sessions, when the adults of the parish have the opportunity to explore important topics of faith together. As facilitators, you have a very important role in helping implement this program. In addition to guiding small-group conversations, facilitators serve as hosts for our Gathering Sessions by helping create a spirit of welcome and hospitality. During this workshop, we'll focus on your role. We'll talk about ways to effectively lead and guide conversation in adult small groups, and we'll explore ways each of us can contribute to the feeling of welcome and outreach at our sessions.

We begin our time together with prayer. Let's have a moment of quiet as we prepare to listen to a portion of Paul's letter to the Colossians.

(After a pause, a reader comes forward to proclaim Colossians 3:11–17, using a Bible.)

— 📖 —

Reading: Colossians 3:11–17

Here there is not Greek and Jew, circumcision and uncircumcision, barbarian, Scythian, slave, free; but Christ is all and in all.

Put on then, as God's chosen ones, holy and beloved, heartfelt compassion, kindness, humility, gentleness, and patience, bearing with one another and forgiving one another, if one has a grievance against another; as the Lord has forgiven you, so must you also do. And over all these put on love, that is, the bond of perfection. And let the peace of Christ control your hearts, the peace into which you were also called in one body. And be thankful. Let the word of Christ dwell in you richly, as in all wisdom you teach and admonish one another, singing psalms, hymns, and spiritual songs with gratitude in your hearts to God. And whatever you do, in word or in deed, do everything in the name of the Lord Jesus, giving thanks to God the Father through him.

The word of the Lord.

— 📖 —

Response: Thanks be to God.

Leader: Loving God,
We thank you for your presence here among us.
Be with us as we begin this journey in faith together.
Bless our gatherings with a spirit of hospitality and
      welcome.
Help us serve with compassion, kindness, humility,
      gentleness, and patience.
Send us your Spirit so that we may listen to all who come
      with open hearts.
Grace us with peaceful and thankful hearts.
We pray this in the name of Jesus, our teacher and friend.
Amen.

PRESENTATION

This is an exciting time! We are beginning a journey of faith that offers all of us wonderful opportunities to deepen our relationship with God and with one another.

Participants

Through the coming year, we will invite adults in our parish to take part in a series of five Gathering Sessions.

(Mention the people who will be participating in the Gathering Sessions—parents of children in the program, catechists, teachers in the Catholic school, etc.)

Theme for the year

These sessions offer the adults in this parish the opportunity to explore important topics of faith together. This year, we will take time to ask ourselves, "What does it mean to be Catholic?" We will explore Catholic thought and Church teaching, and we will continually ask ourselves this important question: In what ways does our Catholic faith make a difference to the way we live our lives? Although each of these gatherings has a somewhat different focus, all of them are designed to enhance our understanding of our faith as adult Catholics.

Role of facilitators

Your role as facilitators in these Gathering Sessions is crucial. Facilitators help participants engage in meaningful conversation with one another. Providing an opportunity for conversation is essential for effective adult faith formation. Adults learn best about their faith by being in conversation with other adults about things that matter to them. Adults also learn by listening to others talk about their own stories and experiences. That is the purpose of small-group conversation.

Overview of catechetical model

Let me give you an overview of what our Gathering Sessions will be like. As a whole, the movement of each Gathering Session evokes this dynamic of invitation and response.

Engage

◆ We gather our thoughts and ideas around a theme that is a point of entry into our Catholic tradition and to our awareness of God's presence in our lives.

Explore

◆ In the Scriptures and Tradition, we hear God's invitation to relationship and to an apprenticeship to Jesus. And we hear that same invitation in the day-to-day experience of people in our faith community.

Reflect
- Our response to this invitation is first prayer—prayer of gratitude for God's invitation, prayer for increased awareness of God's presence in our lives, in the lives of those around us, and in the world.

Respond
- Our response also is to ask, "So what?" So, what does this mean for my life; for my relationship with my family; for how I make decisions at work, at home, or with my friends?

Role of small-group conversation

Small-group conversation plays a vital role in giving adults the opportunity to connect the teachings and traditions of the Catholic Church and the message of the Gospel with their own faith and life experiences. Facilitators help people make these connections.

Focus of conversation

This discussion time offers us the chance to explore very important questions.

- How does my experience relate to (or not relate to) the information presented tonight?
- How do the experiences and thoughts of other people affect my understanding?
- In light of my understanding of this issue, how do I live my life? What am I called to do?
- What questions am I left with?

Gifts of a facilitator

Most importantly, the role of the facilitators is to help create a spirit of welcome and hospitality at our Gathering Sessions and lead or guide the conversations in small groups. How do facilitators do this? What kind of qualifications or gifts does a facilitator need?

Welcoming
- First of all, small-group facilitators are people who enjoy making others feel welcome and at ease. Facilitators are good listeners—people who can get others to talk about their experiences and share their stories.

Open and respectful of differences
- Facilitators also need to be open and respectful of different points of view and have a sense of humor.
- Most importantly, facilitators are people who are excited about continuing to grow in their own faith. This excitement can be contagious and sets a powerful example for our entire parish about the importance of lifelong faith formation.

Facilitator as host

As a facilitator, your main role at our gatherings is that of a host. Think of our sessions as special gatherings, or parties, for guests you care about, guests with whom you want to connect, guests who have valuable stories to share. How do you serve as a good host for these parties?

Preparation	**Prepare well.** As a facilitator, try to arrive at least 15 minutes before the Gathering Session begins so that you can prepare to welcome the guests. Take time to review the key points of the presentation noted on the session handout and the questions to help guide conversation.
Welcome	**Welcome the guests.** Welcome people as they arrive. Remember that your energy and presence will set a hospitable and gracious tone for the gathering.
Importance of conversation	**Serve something you think the guests will enjoy.** Think of the prayer and presentation at our sessions as the meal we are serving our guests. An important part of any party is the conversation that takes place around the meal. As a facilitator, you will help draw out and guide that conversation.
Introductions among participants	**Help guests introduce themselves and make connections with one another.** When people gather in your small group, begin by welcoming them. Thank them for coming and invite them to introduce themselves to one another. (Never skip introductions. Unless you are completely sure, never assume everyone knows everyone.) In addition to giving their name, ask the participants to tell a little about themselves. For example, ask them to tell a little about their family or how long they have been in the parish. This exchange helps enhance a sense of community and fosters a sense of belonging and connection.
Encouraging conversation	**Get the conversation rolling.** After the introductions, lead into the first question on the first page of your session handout. After you have asked the first question, take a breath and be still. People need a bit of time to gather their thoughts before they speak. Gradually, work your way through the questions. If the questions on the handout don't seem to be generating conversation or evoking good responses, add some of your own questions. (You may wish to jot down additional questions during the presentation.)

Addressing questions

Don't feel you have to be an expert.
As the conversation gets going, people may ask the facilitator questions such as "Why does the Church teach this?" or "When did this change occur in the Church?" These are great questions, but it's not up to the facilitator to have all the answers. If someone in the group poses a question and looks to you for an answer, respond by saying, "That's a great question." Open it up to the full group. After that, ask the person if he or she would like you to bring the question to the full group after the small-group conversation. You could also offer to pass the question along to a member of the parish staff.

Noting key ideas

Keep track of key points.
As conversation continues, keep track of important questions, comments, and insights to report back to the large group after the time for small-group discussion ends. This way, everyone at the session will benefit from hearing some of the highlights of your group's conversation.

Bringing groups to closure

Bring the conversation to a close.
At the end of small-group time, take time to put closure to the conversation. Acknowledge the experience of the group. ("Well, we could have used more time . . . " or "We had a lot of different opinions expressed tonight.") An excellent way to close the small-group time is to look people in the eye and thank them for participating. If anyone in your small group has expressed concerns about something in the parish, offer to pass that concern or comment on to a member of the parish staff. This outreach is important and helps people feel connected with the parish.

Before continuing, let me pause and ask this: Given what I have said thus far, what do you think will be the most challenging part of your role as facilitator?

Pair up with someone and take three or four minutes to discuss your responses to this question.

(When participants have had a chance to share ideas with one another, continue with the presentation.)

In closing, let's go over a few points that are important for facilitators to remember as we engage in this important service and ministry.

Dos and don'ts of
small-group conversation

Important Reminders for Small-Group Facilitators
Avoid dominating the group by telling too many of your own stories or controlling the discussion. (It can be very helpful to offer some of your own insights or experiences, but your main priority is to help draw the stories out of others.)

Avoid too casual an attitude where you allow the group to wander without direction.

Keep communication open. Use questions rather than statements. For example, say, "Thanks for your comments, Anne. May we hear from someone else now?" instead of "Okay, Anne, I think you've had enough time."

Be comfortable with silence. Give people time and space to think. Give the Holy Spirit room to move.

Prepare for sessions through prayer and reflection and by looking over the handout ahead of time.

Remember your role as host. You are . . .

- **The Great Entertainer** The energy comes from you. You help create an atmosphere of hospitality and welcome!
- **The Diplomat** Acknowledge conflict and different points of view. Bring closure to the discussion. Season the conversation with a little humor.
- **The Organizer** Be on time and be prepared.
- **The Linguist** Be fluent in all sorts of language—spoken and unspoken.

Above all, be gracious and welcoming. As the opening of the Bishops' document on adult faith formation states,

To be effective ministers of adult faith formation we will first, like Jesus, join people in their daily concerns and walk side by side with them on the pathway of life. We will ask them questions and listen attentively as they speak of their joys, hopes, griefs, and anxieties. (OHWB, 8)

Let's continue to explore the role of the facilitator in small-group conversation. Gather together in groups of four or five. Ask one person to serve as the facilitator (it's great practice). Then refer to the questions on the first page of your handout to help guide your conversation.

As always, begin with introductions and tell a little about yourself. Tell other members of the group why you are serving as a facilitator in this program and what you hope to gain from the experience. Then work through the other questions.

We will spend about 20 minutes in conversation and then move to the next part of the night. Be sure that your group's facilitator writes down any questions people have.

Enjoy yourselves. Thank you!

(If possible, the leader of the workshop and any members of the parish staff who are present should join the small-group conversations.)

(When 15 minutes have passed, make a brief announcement telling the groups it is time to wrap things up. When 20 minutes have passed, call the groups together and invite them to share significant insights, comments, suggestions, and questions. If time allows, discuss responses to the small-group scenarios on the handout on page 48 with the larger group.)

(Thank the participants for their time and commitment and invite everyone to stay for refreshments. Then draw the gathering to a close.)

We have so much to be grateful for—especially for the commitment, the faith, and the energy of all of you who have gathered with us. Before we close, let us take a few moments of quiet to reflect on this time we've had together. In your heart, give thanks for the people gathered here, the stories that were told, and the insights that were shared.

(Pause for a moment to allow silent reflection.)

As we journey together in faith this year, we pray that our hearts will be open to the creativity of God, the love of Jesus, and the wisdom of the Holy Spirit. To conclude our gathering, please pray with me the "Prayer for a Questioning Heart" on the last page of your facilitator handouts.

Facilitator Workshop

The people who serve as facilitators of small-group conversations play a key role in the successful implementation of the faith formation experiences offered in this program. In each of the Gathering Sessions, small-group conversation provides opportunities for adult participants to connect the message of the Gospel and teachings of the Church with their own faith and life experiences. Facilitators help participants make these connections. In addition to leading small-group discussions, facilitators help host the Gathering Sessions by fostering a spirit of hospitality and welcome.

Conversation

◆ Introduce yourself. Tell a little about yourself and about why you decided to serve as a facilitator in this program. What is it that you hope to experience in this program this year?

◆ Name something from the presentation that you found interesting or helpful—something you think is important and want to remember.

◆ Think about a time when you were a newcomer at a gathering. For example, at a new job, at a new school for your children, at a neighborhood gathering, or at a party with your spouse's co-workers. Talk about things others did that made you feel welcomed and at ease. Or talk about what others did (or didn't do) that made you feel disconnected and ill at ease.

◆ What are some specific ways facilitators and parish staff can help make participants at these Gathering Sessions feel welcomed? Be specific and have the facilitator write down your ideas to share with the larger group.

◆ Think about your own experience with small groups. What kinds of situations could arise in small-group conversations that would be challenging or difficult for a facilitator to handle? Have the facilitator write these situations down.

◆ What questions do you have? Have the facilitator write these down.

The Facilitator's Responsibilities

Hospitality Plus

Facilitators offer welcome and hospitality to the participants in this adult faith formation program. It is important to arrive at least 15 minutes before each session begins. This helps us catch our breath and get in place before our guests arrive. We work together to create an atmosphere that is gracious and friendly.

Small-Group Conversation

Facilitators greet people as they move into small groups. Always begin with introductions. Never assume everyone knows everyone else. Help people connect with one another.

Getting the Conversation Rolling

After the introductions, it is time to invite people to talk about the prayer and presentation and how the experience or message relates to their personal experience. Lead into the first question. After you have asked the first question, take a breath and be still. People need a bit of time to gather their thoughts before they speak. If the questions on the handout don't seem to be working, have a few of your own ready. (Some facilitators jot down additional questions during the presentation.)

Small-Group Facilitator Qualifications
Facilitators are people who . . .

- enjoy making others feel welcome,

- are good listeners—who can get others to talk to their experiences and share their stories,

- are open and respectful of different points of view,

- have a sense of humor, and

- desire to continue to grow in their own faith understanding.

Bringing the Conversation to a Close

At the end of small-group discussion, take time to bring closure to the group experience. Acknowledge the experience of the group. ("Well, we could have used more time . . . " or "We had a lot of different opinions expressed and generated some good questions!") An excellent way to close the small-group time is to look people in the eye and thank them for participating. If anyone in your small group is concerned about something in the parish, offer to pass that concern or comment on to a member of the parish staff. This outreach is important and helps people feel connected with the parish.

Small Group Hints: What to Do If . . .

1. The group cannot get started

- Rephrase the discussion question. Ask the question(s) in a different way.
- Read aloud all or part of the descriptive paragraph(s) featured on the front page of your handout.
- Skip whatever is bogging the group down and go on to something else.
- Jot down additional questions during the presentation.

2. Someone dominates

- Say, "Excuse me, Jean. Before you continue, may I ask if anyone else has a comment on this point?"
- Say, "Thanks, Bob. What do other people think?"

3. The group gets off the topic

- State the problem directly: "I think we have moved away from our topic."
- Say: "That's interesting, but how do you react to . . . (restate the question)."

4. The discussion becomes too heated

- Get as many viewpoints as possible from all members of the group.
- State what is happening: "It's obvious we have different opinions here."
- Jot down a brief recap and move on to the next question or topic.

5. Interest lags

- Be sure it is truly lagging. People may just need some time to collect their thoughts.
- Have additional questions ready to use or refer to the other pages of the handout to generate discussion.

6. Some members of the group have not spoken yet

- Say, "Does anyone who has not had the opportunity to speak care to comment?"
- Say, "Dorothy, what do you think?"
- Some adults may be uncomfortable speaking in small groups. If this is the case, make clear that it is okay to participate by listening. If someone says during the introductions, "I'm pretty much a listener—not a talker," respect and accept his or her position.

Sample Small-Group Scenarios

◆ What is the major issue facing each of these groups?

◆ How could a facilitator respond and help get things back on track?

Scenario 1: Silence

The group is sluggish. Jeff is the facilitator and asks members to introduce themselves. After introductions are made, Jeff asks the first question. No one responds. Jeff rewords the question and asks it again. Not a word is said. Most of the members of the group are staring down at the floor. If you were Jeff, what would you do?

Scenario 2: Up Close and Personal

The topic of the session is forgiveness, and the presentation has raised a number of personal issues for Janet, whose father died recently. At the beginning of the group discussion, Janet is very quiet. Then someone says, "I think it is so important to ask for forgiveness from those we love. It is hard to do, but if you don't, the pain will just grow and grow." Suddenly, Janet bursts into tears. "I never got a chance to tell my father that I forgive him," she cries. If you were the facilitator, how would you respond?

Scenario 3: Gossip

The group discussion is lively and animated. Then one person says, "Did you hear what happened at school last week?" She proceeds to talk about a discipline situation and names the students involved. Not only is this off the topic, but it is inappropriate to share with the group. If you were the facilitator, how would you respond?

Prayer for a Questioning Heart

It seems to me Lord
that we search
much too desperately
for answers
when a good question
holds as much grace
as an answer.

Jesus
you are the Great Questioner
Keep our questions alive
that we may always be seekers
rather than settlers.

Guard us well
from the sin of settling in
with our answers
hugged to our breasts.

Make of us
a wondering
far-sighted
questioning
restless people
And give us the feet of pilgrims
on this journey unfinished.

Seasons of Your Heart: Prayers and Reflections
Macrina Wiederkehr, O.S.B.

© Loyola Press

SESSION

A

God's Invitation and Our Response

At the heart of our understanding of God is the dynamic interaction of God's invitation and our response. From the time of the patriarchs and the prophets, we are told again and again that it is God's invitation that deepens the relationship between God and human beings. God's invitation is spoken most clearly in Jesus Christ—it is in Jesus that we get a sense of the depth of relationship to which God is calling us.

Our response to this invitation is faith and an openness to participate in the many ways God's presence is made known to us. For Catholics, this response is shaped and supported by our Catholic faith and by our participation in the faith community.

Leader's 3-Minute Retreat

As you prepare for this Gathering Session, pause for a moment. Take a few deep breaths and be aware of God's loving presence with you.

Read the excerpt from Psalm 139, then call to mind a time when you were particularly aware of God's presence and invitation in your life.

- ◆ Perhaps it was in relation to a career decision or a renewed sense of vocation.
- ◆ Maybe you were aware of God's invitation to take a risk or the reassurance of God's presence in a difficult time.
- ◆ Or maybe you were simply aware of God's presence in nature and creation.

Take time to recall this experience and your response.

For Your Reflection

We often become so busy in our work that we can forget to take time to listen for God's invitation in our own lives. What are a couple of things you would like to do to help yourself become more aware of God's presence throughout the day?

> LORD,
>   you have probed me,
>   you know me:
> you know
>   when I sit and stand;
> you understand my
>   thoughts from afar.
> My travels
>   and my rest you mark;
> with all my ways
>   you are familiar.
> Even before a word
>   is on my tongue,
> LORD,
>   you know it all.
> Behind and before
>   you encircle me
>   and rest your hand
>   upon me.

Psalm 139:1–5

Overview and Agenda

Central Theme

At the heart of our understanding of God is the dynamic interaction of God's invitation and our response. Our response to this invitation is faith and an openness to grow in awareness of God's presence in our lives and in the lives of our families.

Objectives

This session is designed to

◆ examine the dynamic at the heart of our relationship with God, that of invitation-response.

◆ invite participants to discuss the ways in which they are aware of God's presence in their lives.

◆ explore the way our Catholic faith supports us in our response to God.

Schedule

	Arrival and Greetings
10 minutes	Engage
40 minutes	Explore
20 min	Presentation
20 min	Small-group conversation
10 minutes	Reflect and Respond
	Refreshments

To Do Before the Gathering Session

☐ Read the general information on planning and conducting the sessions (page 32).

☐ Identify special groups in the parish to invite to this session. This session might be especially appropriate for members of the religious education committee or advisory board as well as the Parish Council.

☐ Ask two parishioners to prepare to read alternate verses of Psalm 139:1–18.

☐ Ask three parishioners to prepare to read Genesis 17:1–7 and the roles of the narrator and Abraham (Reader Script). Try to choose people with a flair for the dramatic.

☐ Set out the handout packet for distribution as people arrive.

Background for the Presenter

God invites us The dynamics of God's invitation and our human response is at the heart of Catholic life and faith. The writers of the *Catechism of the Catholic Church* begin the examination of the profession of faith by affirming that God never ceases to draw all human beings to himself. It is only in acknowledging and responding to that invitation that human beings find truth and fulfillment (*CCC* 27).

Jesus as model Throughout the Gospels, the effect of Jesus' invitation to a relationship with God is seen in the transformed lives of those who believed. This invitation comes to us today especially through our call to be faithful members of the Catholic Church.

Our response As Catholics, we are called to respond to God's invitation. Fostering an awareness of God's presence in our lives is the first step. Our response is marked by willingness to bring our lives ever more closely into alignment with God's hopes for us. Through our membership in the Church and participation in the sacraments, our openness to God's presence and our ability to respond is strengthened.

ENGAGE

(Adjust the wording as necessary for your group.)

It is good to come together for this year's first Gathering Session. These sessions are just as their name suggests: the opportunity to "gather" on several different levels.

Why we gather: as adults, as parents, as parish members

- We gather as **adults** to deepen our own faith.
- We gather as **parents** who want to pass on the faith to their children.
- And we gather as **parish members** to pray, learn, and go forth together.

Central theme: What does it mean to be Catholic?

The year's theme question is What does it mean to be Catholic? During the year, we will be exploring the contribution Catholic thought and theology make to our understanding of core themes: God, Jesus, the Church, Prayer, and Morality.

Session topic: God's invitation and our response

The topic for this session is God's Invitation and Our Response. At the heart of a Catholic understanding of God is the dynamic interaction of God's invitation and our response.

To gather our thoughts together, let's take a moment for prayer. Reflect on any way God has been especially present to you today. How would you like to respond to God for that gift?

(Pause for a moment to allow silent reflection.)

David's profound awareness of God's presence

Now listen to the way the psalmist David describes his awareness of God's presence and invitation. Can you get a sense of David's awareness of God's presence in his life? And his response of gratitude?

(Have two readers proclaim Psalm 139:1–18 from a Bible, reading alternate verses. Having quiet music playing in the background enhances the reflective tone.)

— 📖 —

Reading: Psalm 139:1–18

LORD, *you have probed me, you know me:*
you know when I sit and stand;
you understand my thoughts from afar.
My travels and my rest you mark;
with all my ways you are familiar.
Even before a word is on my tongue,
LORD, *you know it all.*
Behind and before you encircle me

Behind and before you encircle me
and rest your hand upon me.
Such knowledge is beyond me,
far too lofty for me to reach.

Where can I hide from your spirit?
From your presence, where can I flee?
If I ascend to the heavens, you are there;
if I lie down in Sheol, you are there too.
If I fly with the wings of dawn
and alight beyond the sea,
Even there your hand will guide me,
your right hand hold me fast.
If I say, "Surely darkness shall hide me,
and night shall be my light"—
Darkness is not dark for you,
and night shines as the day.
Darkness and light are but one.

You formed my inmost being;
you knit me in my mother's womb.
I praise you, so wonderfully you made me;
wonderful are your works!
My very self you knew;
my bones were not hidden from you,
When I was being made in secret,
fashioned as in the depths of the earth.
Your eyes foresaw my actions;
in your book all are written down;
my days were shaped, before one came to be.

How precious to me are your designs, O God;
how vast the sum of them!
Were I to count, they would outnumber the sands;
to finish, I would need eternity.

— 📖 —

With David, we too are able to reflect on times in our lives when we have been particularly aware of God's presence, of God's invitation to relationship.

Invitation to participate in this Gathering Session

Your presence here is in response to an invitation—an invitation from the parish, from the people engaged in faith formation, from the whole parish staff.

A formal invitation usually has "RSVP" on it, asking you to respond to the invitation. Can you come? Will you be there?

Before you respond, you probably check to see what your schedule looks like. But you probably also think about whether it is important for you to be there, about what you think is going to happen, and perhaps about what you hope will happen.

Reasons for responding
to that invitation

So, how about this invitation? Take a minute and think about your reaction to the invitation to participate in this Gathering Session. What made you decide to respond positively to the invitation? What do you think is going to take place during this session? What do you hope will take place?

Reflection and conversation

Take just a couple of minutes and turn to someone near you—perhaps someone you don't know or don't know well. Begin by introducing yourself and then talk a bit about your response to the invitation to be here today. Why did you choose to come to this Gathering Session? What do you hope will take place?

*(Give participants a chance to talk with one another.
Call the group back together after three minutes.
If it is feasible, invite some participants to share
their responses with the larger group.)*

EXPLORE

We build relationships through invitation and response.

Invitation and response are part of our everyday lives. They're part of the way in which we get to know one another, build relationships. Both the invitation and the response (whether it is positive or not) say something about the people involved and their relationship.

God's presence is all around us. This presence is itself the invitation.

Invitation and response are also important in our relationship with God. God's presence is all around us, inviting us to be in relationship with God. In the psalm that was part of our opening prayer, David speaks eloquently of the reality of God's presence. David knew that God's presence is itself the invitation.

> *Even before a word is on my tongue,*
> *LORD, you know it all.*
> *Behind and before you encircle me*
> *and rest your hand upon me.*

God's invitation and our response is the central dynamic of the Scriptures and is foundational to Catholic thought and teaching.

The psalm points to our awareness of God's presence. Before we were ever conscious of it, God has been present, protecting, guiding, and inviting us into an ever-deepening relationship.

And, really, this is the theme that weaves together the stories of the Scriptures and is foundational to Catholic thought and teaching.

God's presence is all around us, inviting us into a close relationship. Today we will look at three main points, or characteristics, of that invitation.

God's covenant with Abraham was formed through invitation and response.

In the book of Genesis, the first book of the Bible, we hear how God formed a covenant with Abraham and made him the Patriarch—the father and leader—of the Jewish people. Simply put, this is the story of God's invitation and Abraham's response. Each incident in the story shows Abraham's growing awareness of God's presence in his life and the importance of his response to God.

At the beginning of the story, Abraham and his wife, Sarah, were living a pretty good life in a place called Haran (hair un). They had servants, animals, tents, and all the modern conveniences of 2000 B.C.

God calls Abraham.

Then one day, God showed up and told them to pack their things and move to a place he would show them. How did Abraham and Sarah respond?

Promise of the relationship between God and his people

Abraham and Sarah didn't bat an eye. They didn't put up an argument. They didn't ask *when* or *where* or *why us*. They just gathered all the servants and the animals and the household goods and did what God wanted. In return, God promised to bless Abraham and his descendants and to make them a great nation.

Promise to Abraham to be the father of a great nation

Over the years, God promised Abraham again and again that he would be the father of a great people. Abraham stayed faithful to God, but he couldn't help getting a bit skeptical about the promise. After all, he and Sarah were childless— and they were getting old.

In the 17th chapter of Genesis, we learn about the fulfillment of God's promise to Abraham. When Abraham was 99 years old, God once again invited him to become the father of a great people. How did Abraham respond?

Abraham's response to God's invitation

(Ask the readers to stand and read to the group the Genesis story and Abraham's reflection from the Reader Script.)

— 🕊 —

(This script is found on page 61–62. The reading should take three to four minutes.)

— 🕊 —

Characteristic 1: God consistently invites us to be more than we think we are. We hear this invitation through the Catholic Church.

The story of Abraham shows us the first characteristic of God's invitations: God consistently invites people not only to be more than they think they *are* but also to be more than they think they *can be*. Abraham was invited to leave his quiet life as a herdsman and set out on a journey that had no clear end point. Because of his trusting response to God, Abraham in his old age became not only the father of Isaac but also "the father of a host of nations," just as God had promised.

In many ways, as we look to the people in the Scriptures, the saints in our Catholic Tradition, and the faithful people around us, we can recognize this as a hallmark of an invitation from God. God calls us through the Church to be more than we think we can be: to be more loving, more just, more courageous, more gentle, more of a leader, more willing to listen.

Characteristic 2:
God expects a response.

The second characteristic of God's invitation is this: It's not enough simply to be aware of that invitation; we must *act* on it as well. We must respond!

Jesus is the ultimate expression of God's invitation and human response.

At the heart of Catholic identity is a close personal relationship with Jesus Christ. It is in Jesus that we, as Catholics, find the ultimate expression of God's invitation and human response. In the person of Jesus, both invitation and response are given full expression.

Jesus consistently invited people to respond to God's promise of new life.

The example of Jesus' call to the apostles

During his ministry, Jesus consistently invited people to go beyond themselves—to go beyond what they (and others) thought they were capable of doing and to embrace God's promise of new life in him. Jesus' ministry began with his invitation to Peter, James, John, and the others who would be formed into his apostles. They were invited to leave their jobs and follow him. And they did! The call of Jesus was an invitation for them to be more than they were, more than they thought they could be. And their positive response to Jesus' invitation, "Come and follow me!" is the foundation of their participation in Jesus' ministry and the continuation of that ministry in the Church.

The story of Zacchaeus also stands out as an example of the power of God's invitation.

Another person who responded to Jesus' invitation was Zacchaeus. His story presents a great example of how powerful God's invitation really is.

You remember Zacchaeus—a little guy, a tax collector, kept to himself a lot, had few friends but plenty of money. I doubt that when Zacchaeus got up that morning and set off for work he had any idea what the day was going to bring. But I would imagine that for the rest of his life Zacchaeus had reason to reflect often on that day's events.

As he cut through the market, he heard that Jesus was passing through town. "Jesus . . . Jesus . . . I know I know that name," he thought to himself as he became more aware of the excitement and anticipation in the air.

Zacchaeus followed the crowd that was gathering along the dusty road to see Jesus. Being short, Zacchaeus couldn't see over the crowd; being resourceful, he ran ahead and climbed a tree in order to see Jesus.

Jesus' invitation to Zacchaeus couldn't have been clearer: "Zacchaeus, come down quickly, for today I must stay at your house."

Can you imagine Zacchaeus' response to that invitation? He was probably lucky he didn't fall out of the tree! Luke tells us that Zacchaeus scrambled down and welcomed Jesus with joy.

But that joy must have been dimmed for a moment as he heard many of those around him whispering, but loudly enough for him to hear. They were saying things like "Jesus must not know who that guy is." "Surely Jesus wouldn't stay in the tax collector's house. He must be mistaken." "Jesus has gone to stay in the house of a sinner!"

But it was Jesus' invitation—Jesus calling Zacchaeus to be more than he thought he could be, certainly more than the town's people thought—that gave Zacchaeus the courage and confidence to respond. And to respond with renewed faith and hope and charity. The Gospel of Luke has Zacchaeus proclaim, "Behold, half of my possessions, Lord, I shall give to the poor, and if I have extorted anything from anyone I shall repay it four times over."

This is the response that Jesus asks for and that God's invitation demands—one of confidence in God's presence and willingness to further his plan.

Characteristic 3: Our response is faith in God's presence and willingness to further God's plan.

So this is the third characteristic of the invitation-response relationship: Our response is faith in God's presence and willingness to further God's plan. Think of the examples we've looked at today.

Think of Abraham's great faith and his willingness to do whatever God wanted him to do. Think of the apostles, leaving their families and jobs to become faithful followers of Jesus. And think of how Zacchaeus responded courageously to Jesus' invitation to become better than he thought he could be.

Review of three core characteristics

The life-giving relationship between God's invitation and our response permeates our lives as Catholics. God's invitation calls us beyond our fears and concerns to a life that is shaped by an assurance of God's presence and a confidence in God's love for us.

And with the invitation is the necessity of response—RSVP! Our response takes the shape of a change of heart and a change of life. We grow in our awareness of God around us and in our willingness to proclaim in action and word the reality of God's presence and hope for the world.

But how do we experience God's presence?

57

It may seem the disciples and even Zacchaeus had it easy— they could see Jesus and hear his call. But how do we hear that invitation?

On the very human, everyday level, we are aware of God's invitation in the people and events and world around us

- in the friend who listens to our struggles and expresses confidence in our ability to work them through,
- in the person who wants to confide in us on the day when we have no time and little patience to spare,
- or in the child who calls down for one more glass of water after we've had a busy and tiring day.

We experience God's presence in our families.

We can be keenly aware of God's presence within our families. We sense his presence in a laughing child, a caring spouse, a sleeping infant. And we respond with grateful hearts by caring for our families and giving special attention to the bonds of love that unite us and connect us with God.

We can experience God's presence in society.

We can experience God's invitation in the society around us, particularly in those who are less fortunate than ourselves. We respond by caring for others, by sharing our resources with them, and by working to overcome the structures that oppress.

We experience God's presence in the Church, particularly in the Eucharist.

For Catholics, these experiences are clarified and celebrated within our parishes, especially in the Eucharist. As we gather each week to celebrate the Mass, we experience the presence of God in the people we celebrate with, in the Scriptures as they are proclaimed, and in the Eucharist itself as the continuing expression of the presence of the risen Jesus under the appearance of bread and wine. It is in these celebrations that we are given the grace (God's life and love) to grow in our awareness of God's call and to respond with openness to this invitation to live in God's love.

Invitation and response: how do they come to expression in your life? Let's move into small groups to continue this conversation.

(Small-group conversation)

(Invite participants to form groups of 6 or 7, including a facilitator. Explain that the groups will have 15 minutes for conversation on the points outlined on the first page of the handout.)

(As the time for small-group conversation comes to a close, invite the participants to bring their attention back to the full group. Invite the small-group facilitators to share insights from their groups.)

REFLECT

(Instrumental music playing softly in the background enhances the sense of prayerfulness.)

(Pause briefly at each / mark.)

We've been doing a lot of talking. Let's take a moment now to quiet ourselves and rest in God's presence.

Close your eyes if you'd like and pay attention to the rhythm of your breathing. / Know that it is God who breathes life into you, / who holds you in existence, / who loves you beyond imagination, / who waits for your loving response. / God already knows what is in your heart, but he wants to hear it from you. / What would you like to say to him?

(Allow time for personal reflection.)

Please respond, "We thank you, God!"

> Let us pray.
> For the wonders of creation.
>   (We thank you, God!)
> For the love of our families.
>   (We thank you, God!)
> For the gift of our Catholic faith.
>   (We thank you, God!)
> For the support of our Church community.
>   (We thank you, God!)
> For your constant and loving presence.
>   (We thank you, God!)

Loving God, we are grateful for the gift of this time together, for the stories told, for the insights shared. Help us to deepen our faith by opening our eyes and our hearts to the signs of your invitation in our lives. We pray this in the name of Jesus, your Son, who teaches us how to live and how to love. Amen.

RESPOND

We've talked about many ways that we can respond to God's invitation. Two of the most important are by passing on our faith to our children and by deepening our own understanding of God's presence and love. The handouts will give you some ideas of how to achieve those responses.

(Refer to the handouts photocopied from pages 64–66.)

"Bringing the Message into Everyday Life" outlines the importance of taking time every day to reflect on that day's events and to think about how we have responded to God's invitation. As adults, we need to consciously examine that response. Just paying attention tonight isn't enough. We must carry tonight's message home and practice it every day.

"Bringing the Message Home" contains a few paragraphs by Tom McGrath. Tom is a Catholic and a father who writes and speaks about family life and spirituality. I think you'll find his words both interesting and inspiring. The handout also lists suggestions of things that families can do together to respond to God's invitation.

"Deepening the Message" is for your personal reflection on the sacramentality of our world and what that means for us.

That concludes our session. Thank you for your attention and participation. I hope we will see you all back next time *(name the date and time)* when we focus on the person of Jesus and our response to the question Jesus asked his disciples: "Who do you say that I am?"

READER SCRIPT
The Biblical Account of God's Invitation

— 📖 —

Reader 1:   **A Reading from Genesis 17:1–7:**
When Abram was ninety-nine years old, the LORD appeared to him and said: "I am God the Almighty. Walk in my presence and be blameless. Between you and me I will establish my covenant, and I will multiply you exceedingly."

When Abram prostrated himself, God continued to speak to him: "My covenant with you is this: you are to become the father of a host of nations. No longer shall you be called Abram; your name shall be Abraham, for I am making you the father of a host of nations. I will render you exceedingly fertile; I will make nations of you; kings shall stem from you. I will maintain my covenant with you and your descendants after you throughout the ages as an everlasting pact, to be your God and the God of your descendants after you."

— 📖 —

Reader 2:   What was Abraham's response? The Scriptures tell us that Abraham
(as narrator)   fell down to the ground laughing when he heard God's promise. Imagine for a moment . . . what do you think was going through Abraham's mind? Maybe it was something like this . . .

READER SCRIPT
Abraham's Reflections on God's Invitation

Reader 3:
(as Abraham) God, I'm sorry to laugh, really. And I mean no disrespect, but come *on*—a father of nations? How can that be? I am 99 years old, and Sarah is 90—and, well . . . Isn't it *obvious*? You know we are too old to have children!

Oh, we've had a good life, God. And I thank *you* for that. So many promises you've made to Sarah and to me—and you've kept every one. Well, except this one. But isn't it too late for this? We are old now. We can't have children anymore. A father of nations—what a blessing that would be. But there is one little, tiny, small detail you seem to be forgetting. The children, God . . . where are the children?

For years, years, we have followed you. And you have shown us your love in many ways. But children, God—well, frankly, I just don't see *how* it can be done. I can't imagine it! It is impossible! *(Pause)* Isn't it?

Oh, I suppose *anything* is possible with you, God—but children? And what will Sarah say? I know Sarah—she'll laugh me right out of the tent! But Sarah is a good woman, a faithful woman, and she loves *you* very much, God. She will trust you. I know she will. She always has.

That's it, isn't it God? Faith and trust. I don't know how you are going to pull this off, but maybe I don't need to know. I just need to have faith that you can.

I hear your voice, God, inside my heart, calling me, inviting me to be the father of nations. I will have faith in that promise. You lead, God. I will follow. I need to go to Sarah now. You know, *(look upwards)* it might not hurt if you had a little talk with her yourself. I mean, I could use a little help here.

Sarah and me—parents? Who would have guessed? *(Pause)* I feel younger already!

© Loyola Press

God's Invitation and Our Response

At the heart of our understanding of God is the dynamic interaction of God's invitation and our response. From the time of the patriarchs and the prophets, we are told again and again that it is God's invitation that deepens the relationship between God and human beings. God's invitation is spoken most clearly in Jesus Christ. It is in Jesus that we get a sense of the depth of relationship to which God is calling us.

Our response to this invitation is faith and an openness to participate in the many ways God's presence is made known to us. For Catholics, this response is shaped and supported by our Catholic faith and by our participation in the faith community.

Conversation

When do you feel closest to God? Where do you feel God's presence most strongly?

I feel closest to God

☐ when I gather with my parish community for liturgy.

☐ when I am outside—surrounded by the beauty of nature.

☐ when things are going well.

☐ when I am struggling or experiencing difficult things in my life.

☐ when I work with others to help those who are hungry or homeless.

☐ when I pray with others.

☐ _____

_____

_____

◆ Introduce yourself and talk about one insight or new idea you gained from the presentation.

◆ Take a few minutes to think about the question in the box and then talk about a time when you were aware of God's presence in your life.

◆ Name a way—big or small—in which you responded to God's invitation in your life. What was the situation? How did you respond? What has happened since?

◆ Name some things you could do to deepen or enhance your awareness of God's presence in your life.

© Loyola Press

Bringing the Message into Everyday Life

Part of the rich Tradition of the Catholic Church is the recognition of the need to take time to reflect on the events of the day in order to be more aware of God's presence and invitation to us. This is a time to recognize and remember God's loving care and his hope that we experience the fullness of life. It invites us to reflect on the day's activities, remembering God's invitation and our response—or our lack of response.

Reflecting on the Day: Examen

- **Stillness.** This time of prayer begins by taking a few moments to quiet ourselves and to remember that we are in God's presence. We also ask God to help us to see and to understand the presence of grace (God's life and love) in our lives.

- **Gratitude.** We remember times of contentment or joy or simply pleasure in the day. We give thanks to God for these gifts and for the gift of life.

- **Reflection.** Confident of the Spirit's guidance, we think over the events and experiences of the day. We reflect on the people we encountered and our response to them and to the needs that they may have expressed. We consider the way we reacted to problems or concerns. We try to recognize all of these as invitations from God to deepen our relationship with him and with others.

- **Sorrow.** In looking back on the day, we recognize ways in which we failed to respond or to take action to show our love for God and for others. We may recognize the way the day left little time for us to be aware of God's presence in the people and creation around us. We bring these times to God not for judgment but for healing.

- **Hopefulness.** We conclude by asking God's blessings on the next day and trusting that the Spirit will guide and enlighten us.

Adapted from Margaret Silf,
Inner Compass
Chicago: Loyola Press, 1999

© Loyola Press

Bringing the Message Home

How do parents pass on faith to their children? The following paragraphs are excerpts from the introduction and first chapter of the book *Raising Faith-Filled Kids* by Tom McGrath.

Family life presents ordinary opportunities to nurture children's faith, to introduce them to such building-block concepts as trust, respect, belief, service, love, and reliance on a higher power.

You don't pass on a living faith like a quarterback handing off a football to a running back. And parents don't create faith. Faith comes from God, and God has placed the seed of faith in each child. Parents have a major influential role in how prepared the child is and how well the faith is nurtured. But we don't create faith, possess faith, or control it. Faith is a relationship like the relationship between vine and its branches. Faith flows. *[Parents'] main task is to encourage the flow and not block it.*

There is no formula or prescribed set of actions that will do the trick. There is just living and loving together and taking opportunities to share what you have found to be of great value—your beliefs and practices of living in God's love.

In short, kids get faith by living in a home where faith also dwells.

Discuss with your children how exciting it is to give or receive an invitation to an event such as a birthday party. Explain that Jesus invites us every day to live in his love. Talk about things you can do within your family to answer Jesus' invitation. Here are some suggestions. You may think of others yourselves.

- One way we can answer God's invitation is by going to Mass and receiving the sacraments. Make a commitment to attend Sunday Mass together as a family every week.

- We answer God's invitation when we do things to serve others. Choose something you can do as a family to connect with your parish (serve as greeters at Mass, help with a social function, volunteer with a service project at church).

- Prayer is another way to answer God's invitation. Take time as a family to say grace before meals. Take turns adding personal prayers of thanks or praying for special intentions.

- God gave us our beautiful world. We can answer God's invitation by taking care of that world. Decide as a family on something you can do to care for the earth.

Deepening the Message

"The world is charged with the grandeur of God."
Gerard Manley Hopkins

Think about a time when you were really struck by an awareness of God's presence.

Perhaps it was

- the grandeur of a sunset
- a rainbow on a rainy day
- the beauty of a sleeping child
- the safe return of a loved one
- the hoped-for results on a medical test
- the presence of help after a natural disaster

In response to any of these events, we might express a fervent "Thank God!" Or we might murmur a heartfelt "Thank you, God."

Each of these serves as an effective example of our experience of the "sacramentality of the world." What does that mean?

Sacramentality refers to a central conviction of our Catholic faith that all reality is sacred because it is created and sustained by God. When Ignatius of Loyola, the founder of the Society of Jesus (the Jesuit community), urged his followers to "find God in all things," he was giving voice to this core Catholic belief. We believe that God gives expression to the divine presence

through the ordinary things of life—touch, words, food, water, and so forth.

So, when we talk about being aware of the signs of God's presence and invitation in the world around us and in our relationships, we are appealing to the fundamentally Catholic notion of sacramentality.

Sacraments and sacramentality? How do they fit together? Since God is present in the world around us and in our relationships, does this mean the sacraments have lost their unique role as a source of grace?

Definitely not! Exploring the meaning of the sacraments within this sense of sacramentality enhances and enriches our appreciation of the sacraments. Jesus gave us the sacraments so that we could become even more intensely aware of God's presence in the world. The sacraments celebrate the presence of God that we experience every day. They are the premier expression of God's invitation.

God's invitation and our response of faith are lived out and experienced in our relationships and in our day-to-day lives. We celebrate them in the sacraments.

© Loyola Press

B

"Who Do You Say That I Am?"

"Who do you say that I am?" Two thousand years ago, Jesus asked this question of his disciples and followers. Jesus asks this same question of us today: "Who do you say that I am?"

This is the fundamental Christian question because in naming who Jesus was and how he responded to the world around him, we gain insight into who Jesus is calling us to be. At the heart of Catholic teaching is the conviction that as followers of Jesus, we are called both to know Jesus' teachings and to follow his example in our daily lives. We, too, are called to be teacher, healer, friend, and to share the saving presence of Jesus with one another. As disciples, we are to follow the Master's guide—to live as Jesus lived and to love as Jesus loved.

Leader's 3-Minute Retreat

As you prepare for this Gathering Session, pause for a moment. Take a few deep breaths and be aware of God's loving presence with you.

Prayerfully read this excerpt from Mark's Gospel. What images of the disciples and of Jesus are revealed to you in this story? How might the disciples have heard that question: "Who do you say that I am?" Why do you think Jesus asked it?

For Your Reflection

Reflect back on times in your life when your sense of Jesus' presence has been most clear. In what ways has your image of Jesus changed over the years? How has it stayed the same? As you prepare for this session, take time to give expression to your own personal response to Jesus' question:

Who do you say that I am?

> Now Jesus and his disciples set out for the villages of Caesarea Philippi. Along the way he asked his disciples, "Who do people say that I am?" They said in reply, "John the Baptist, others Elijah, still others one of the prophets." And he asked them, "But who do you say that I am?"
>
> Mark 8:27–29

Overview and Agenda

Central Theme

The Gospels provide various images of Jesus that help believers come to an understanding of who Jesus is in their lives.

Objectives

This session is designed to

◆ highlight the different ways the Gospel writers portrayed Jesus as they attempted to respond to the questions and experiences of their day.

◆ examine some of the images of Jesus that can be found in the Gospels with particular focus on Jesus as Teacher, Healer, Friend, and Savior.

◆ provide an opportunity for adults to reflect on their images of Jesus and the meaning these images have for the way they live.

Schedule

	Arrival and Greetings
10 minutes	Engage
40 minutes	Explore
20 min	Presentation
20 min	Small-group conversation
10 minutes	Reflect and Respond
	Refreshments

To Do Before the Gathering Session

☐ Read the general information on planning and conducting the session (page 32).

☐ Identify special groups in the parish to invite to this session. Bible study groups and parish lectors might be particularly appropriate for this session.

☐ Ask five people to serve as readers for the opening prayer. Mark the Bible for the Gospel reader and make copies of the readers' script for the other four.

☐ Ask six people to serve as readers: four during the Explore section, providing them with the biblical references for their readings; and two during the Reflect section, providing photocopies of the Prayers of Petition.

☐ In the Bible, clearly mark the Gospel passages that the four readers will be proclaiming during the Explore section— Matthew 7:24–29, Mark 2:1–12, John 21:1–14, Luke 4:16–21.

☐ Set out handouts for distribution as people arrive.

Background for the Presenter

At the heart of the Catholic Tradition is the mystery of Christ. All of Church teaching is read in light of this mystery. It is in this sense that we speak of a "hierarchy of truths"; all doctrines are understood in relationship to the foundation (CCC 90).

Compiled several years after the life, death, and resurrection of Jesus, the four Gospels serve as the starting point for our understanding of who Jesus was and who he is for us today. Written from the perspective of several decades, the Gospels portray Jesus the Christ as he was known both in history and through faith. An overly literal reading of the Gospels as historically accurate is confusing (as there are apparent contradictions in details among the Gospels) and limits our ability to recognize the message of the Gospel writers and its application for our lives.

Suggested reading *The Catholic Study Bible* (New York: Oxford University Press, 1990), which includes the *New American Bible* and provides extensive commentary in the opening pages and before each Gospel. For information on the development of the Gospels, see CCC 126. On the fundamental importance of the Gospels for understanding Jesus, refer to CCC 127.

ENGAGE

Welcome, everyone! It is good to come together for this Gathering Session.

A passage from Mark's Gospel is proclaimed, followed by four different reflections on the question: Who do you say that I am?

During our time together our conversation, reflection, and prayer center on the person of Jesus. Two thousand years have passed since Jesus walked the dusty roads of Palestine. At that time, many of the people who knew Jesus, including his friends and his followers, didn't know what to make of him. Some called him a prophet, others thought of him as a miracle worker, a healer. Jesus was known to some as teacher and friend—and to others as Savior, Son of God.

Today, we are faced with the same important question: Who is Jesus to us, and why is he so important? This gathering gives us an opportunity to learn more about Jesus—to spend time together reflecting on his life, his love, and his teaching. We begin in prayer with a reading from the Gospel of Mark:

(A reader comes forward and reads Mark 8:27–29 from a Bible.)

Reading: Mark 8:27–29

Now Jesus and his disciples set out for the villages of Caesarea Philippi. Along the way he asked his disciples, "Who do people say that I am?" They said in reply, "John the Baptist, others Elijah, still others one of the prophets." And he asked them, "But who do you say that I am?"

The Gospel of the Lord.

Response: Praise to you, Lord Jesus Christ.

(The leader and four readers then present the reflections found in the Reader Script. Those who read the reflections can do so from their places.)

EXPLORE

Core question: Who do you say that I am?	Who do you say that I am? The response to that question has been the basis of a good deal of theological writing, prayerful reflection, intense debate, and a Church council or two.
Each of us must answer for ourselves.	Who do you say that I am? Across the centuries, the Catholic Tradition has addressed this question from a wide variety of perspectives, drawing on insights from philosophy, theology, history, biblical studies, the arts, and most recently, the social sciences. But in the end, this is a question that each of us must answer for ourselves. Drawing on the resources of our Catholic faith, we reflect on who Jesus is for us.
Naming who Jesus is gives us a sense of who we are and who we are called to be.	Who do you say that I am? For the Catholic, that isn't merely an interesting question with a complex answer. As followers of Jesus, this is our fundamental question. In naming who Jesus is and how he responded to the world around him, we gain insight into who we are and how we are to live our lives.
	We approach this question from the perspective of the Gospel. What do the Gospel writers tell us about who Jesus is? Before we turn to the Gospels and some of the key images of Jesus that we find there, it is helpful to step back and talk briefly about the nature of the Gospels.
Catholic biblical scholarship	Matthew, Mark, Luke, and John. Each of these Gospels provides us with a particular angle for exploring who Jesus was and who he is for us today. Catholic biblical scholarship has given us a good deal of insight into how and why the Gospels were written, which will be helpful to us in reading them.
	Three points will be particularly helpful for us to remember in this discussion.
Point 1: Gospels compiled long after Jesus' death and resurrection; not designed as accurate chronology	First, the Gospels are not eyewitness accounts. The earliest of them, the Gospel of Mark, was written about 40 years after Jesus' death and resurrection. Although stories about Jesus and collections of his sayings began to circulate fairly early, it wasn't until much later that these stories and sayings were brought together into a cohesive whole. So they were not intended to be an accurate chronology of Jesus' itinerary or a verbatim account of Jesus' teaching. They were meant to portray the life and teaching, the death and resurrection of Jesus, especially to people who hadn't known him personally.

Point 2:
Each Gospel designed for particular group of people with specific questions and concerns

Each Gospel was written in a particular place for a particular group of people. For example, the Gospel of Matthew was written for a community that was primarily Jewish; Luke's for a mainly non-Jewish community. Each writer selected and organized the various stories to respond to the questions, interests, and concerns of his particular audience.

Wedding album example

Imagine that a couple wanted to tell the story of the period between their engagement and the wedding. They asked three friends to take pictures and jot down stories that they could all share together. Now imagine that

- one friend was to make a picture album for the bride's parents (who weren't too sure this guy was good enough for their only daughter),
- the second friend was making one for the groom's parents (who were eager to see their youngest son happily married),
- and the final album was for the couple themselves.

It seems pretty clear that those albums would take on slightly different tones to reflect the interests of the recipients and to address their concerns and feelings.

That is similar to what the Gospel writers did—they pulled together the shared memory of the wider Christian community and wove the stories, images, and sayings of Jesus into an account that would address their particular community and challenge its members to continue to live as followers of Christ.

Point 3:
Gospels told from perspective of faith

And the third point: imagine that the 25th anniversary of the couple whose engagement time was caught in those photo albums is approaching. Now, three more albums are created that take account of the journey of the couple from engagement through the wedding ceremony. But now the stories are told and the pictures arranged from the perspective of 25 years of marriage. The significance of some events and the roles of certain people take on more (or less) meaning in light of the events of the past 25 years.

The same is true for the work of the Gospel writers. Jesus' death and resurrection and the later development of the gathering of believers under the leadership of the apostles and the guidance of the Holy Spirit had taken place and had flourished. So Jesus' death was understood in a new way in light of the resurrection. Also, Jesus' promise to always be with his followers took on new significance when it was fulfilled at Pentecost. The Gospel accounts were written in light of the resurrection and the ongoing inspiration of the Holy Spirit.

Examining four core images

When we look to the Gospels to examine who Jesus was and who Jesus is for us today, we see responses rooted in faith. In many ways, the Gospels are extended responses given by the Gospel writers to the fundamental Christian question: "Who do you say that I am?"

While each Gospel brings a somewhat different perspective, a number of core images are present. We look at four of those key images now: Teacher, Healer, Friend, and Savior.

Teacher

Consistent image of Jesus teaching and preaching

In parables and formal discourse with the crowds and in informal conversation with the disciples as they walked along the road, Jesus was always teaching and preaching a new way of life rooted in the Kingdom of God.

The writer of Matthew's Gospel presents the Sermon on the Mount in which Jesus teaches the Beatitudes and gives teaching on a wide range of topics, including anger, divorce, oaths, almsgiving, and love of enemies. That section ends with this:

(A reader comes forward and reads Matthew 7:24–29 from a Bible.)

— 📖 —

Reading: Matthew 7:24–29

"Everyone who listens to these words of mine and acts on them will be like a wise man who built his house on rock. The rain fell, the floods came, and the winds blew and buffeted the house. But it did not collapse; it had been set solidly on rock. And everyone who listens to these words of mine but does not act on them will be like a fool who built his house on sand. The rain fell, the floods came, and the winds blew and buffeted the house. And it collapsed and was completely ruined."

When Jesus finished these words, the crowds were astonished at his teaching, for he taught them as one having authority, and not as their scribes.

— 📖 —

Jesus as one who taught with authority

So Jesus not only taught, he taught with authority. There wasn't a sense that Jesus was merely passing on a teaching passed down over the centuries. He was teaching the truth he knew because of his unique relationship with God his Father. There was no inconsistency between what Jesus taught and how he lived. And in that rested his authority.

Healer

Healed those who were sick, but also included invitation to conversion

Scattered throughout the Gospels are words like these: "At sunset, all who had people sick with various diseases brought them to him. He laid his hands on each of them and cured them" (Luke 4:40). But often Jesus' healing went beyond physical healing; it also included an invitation to conversion and forgiveness of sin. Here is an example from the Gospel of Mark.

*(A reader comes forward and reads
Mark 2:1–12 from a Bible.)*

— 📖 —

Reading: Mark 2:1–12

When Jesus returned to Capernaum after some days, it became known that he was at home. Many gathered together so that there was no longer room for them, not even around the door, and he preached the word to them. They came bringing to him a paralytic carried by four men. Unable to get near Jesus because of the crowd, they opened up the roof above him. After they had broken through, they let down the mat on which the paralytic was lying. When Jesus saw their faith, he said to the paralytic, "Child, your sins are forgiven." Now some of the scribes were sitting there asking themselves, "Why does this man speak that way? He is blaspheming. Who but God alone can forgive sins?" Jesus immediately knew in his mind what they were thinking to themselves, so he said, "Why are you thinking such things in your hearts? Which is easier, to say to the paralytic, 'Your sins are forgiven,' or to say, 'Rise, pick up your mat and walk'? But that you may know that the Son of Man has authority to forgive sins on earth"—he said to the paralytic, "I say to you, rise, pick up your mat, and go home." He rose, picked up his mat at once, and went away in the sight of everyone. They were all astounded and glorified God, saying, "We have never seen anything like this."

— 📖 —

While the crowds are impressed by the physical healing, it is the spiritual healing that Jesus desires.

Friend

Setting of meals throughout Gospels—hospitality and table fellowship

Throughout the Gospels, we find images of Jesus as friend and companion. In this context, it is worth noting the multiple occasions on which Jesus is found eating with others. The writer of the Gospel of John places hospitality and table fellowship at both the beginning and the end of Jesus' ministry on earth. At the beginning is the wedding at Cana, where Jesus turned water into wine. At the end is this account of Jesus' appearance to the disciples following the resurrection.

*(A reader comes forward and reads
John 21:1–14 from a Bible.)*

— 📖 —

Reading: John 21:1–14

After this, Jesus revealed himself again to his disciples at the Sea of Tiberias. He revealed himself in this way. Together were Simon Peter, Thomas called Didymus, Nathanael from Cana in Galilee, Zebedee's sons, and two others of his disciples. Simon Peter said to them, "I am going fishing." They said to him, "We also will come with you." So they went out and got into the boat, but that night they caught nothing. When it was already dawn, Jesus was standing on the shore; but the disciples did not realize that it was Jesus. Jesus said to them, "Children, have you caught anything to eat?" They answered him, "No." So he said to them, "Cast the net over the right side of the boat and you will find something." So they cast it, and were not able to pull it in because of the number of fish. So the disciple whom Jesus loved said to Peter, "It is the Lord." When Simon Peter heard that it was the Lord, he tucked in his garment, for he was lightly clad, and jumped into the sea. The other disciples came in the boat, for they were not far from shore, only about a hundred yards, dragging the net with the fish. When they climbed out on shore, they saw a charcoal fire with fish on it and bread. Jesus said to them, "Bring some of the fish you just caught." So Simon Peter went over and dragged the net ashore full of one hundred fifty-three large fish. Even though there were so many, the net was not torn. Jesus said to them, "Come, have breakfast." And none of the disciples dared to ask him, "Who are you?" because they realized it was the Lord. Jesus came over and took the bread and gave it to them, and in like manner the fish. This was now the third time Jesus was revealed to his disciples after being raised from the dead.

— 📖 —

Here and throughout the Gospels, Jesus is portrayed as one who cares for his friends and invites them into ever deeper relationship with him and with one another.

Savior

Through Jesus, we gain eternal life; our sins are forgiven; we are saved from all that oppresses us.

The core of our Catholic faith points to Jesus as Savior, the one sent by God to save all of humanity. The image of Jesus as Savior is rooted in our belief that it is through Jesus that we are granted eternal life. It is through Jesus that our sins are forgiven and we are made right with God. But Jesus as Savior is not only a future reality; it is a present one as well. Jesus saves us from all that oppresses us. The writer of Luke's Gospel places this story at the beginning of Jesus' ministry.

*(A reader comes forward and reads
Luke 4:16–21 from a Bible.)*

— 📖 —

Reading: Luke 4:16–21

*He came to Nazareth, where he had grown up, and
went according to his custom into the synagogue on
the sabbath day. He stood up to read and was handed
a scroll of the prophet Isaiah. He unrolled the scroll
and found the passage where it was written:*

*"The Spirit of the Lord is upon me,
because he has anointed me
to bring glad tidings to the poor.
He has sent me to proclaim liberty to captives
and recovery of sight to the blind,
to let the oppressed go free,
and to proclaim a year acceptable to the Lord."*

*Rolling up the scroll, he handed it back to the attendant
and sat down, and the eyes of all in the synagogue
looked intently at him. He said to them, "Today this
scripture passage is fulfilled in your hearing."*

— 📖 —

The call for change of heart and life

Jesus' saving action in the Gospels was an invitation to all to conversion of heart and change of life. Jesus saves people from sin and saves us for the work of serving the Kingdom of God.

We are called to follow Jesus' example:

Jesus as Teacher, Healer, Friend, and Savior. As followers of Jesus, we recognize him in each of these images and recognize in these images the call to follow his example by being teachers, healers, friends, and by sharing the saving presence of Jesus.

. . . as teachers

We are teachers when we teach our children to forgive, to be peacemakers, and to share with others. And we are teachers when our actions give evidence of the values that Jesus lived.

... as healers

We are healers when we care for our children or our aging parents, when we reach out to someone who is hurting emotionally, and when we foster peace in our homes, neighborhoods, and country.

... as friends

Our role as friend is clear when we listen carefully to the concerns and hopes of others, when we reach out to someone new in the community, or when we are simply present to someone experiencing loss or difficult times.

... as those who share the saving work of Jesus.

We share the saving presence of Jesus when we forgive and ask for forgiveness; when we pray with and for someone going through difficult times; and when we work to remedy those situations and structures—in our community and beyond—that fail to support the dignity of all people.

Teacher, Healer, Friend, Savior. Who do you say Jesus is and what does that mean for your life? Let's move into small groups to consider that question.

(Small-group conversation)

(Invite participants to form groups of 6 or 7, including a facilitator. Explain that the groups will have 15 minutes for conversation on the points outlined on the first page of the handout.)

(As the time for small-group conversation comes to a close, invite the participants to bring their attention back to the full group. If time allows, invite the small-group facilitators to share insights from their groups.)

R E F L E C T

*(Instrumental music playing softly in the background
enhances the sense of prayerfulness.)*
(Pause briefly at each / mark.)

We have heard some stories of how Jesus was present to the
people of his time. We have talked about the experiences that
have shaped our own sense of who Jesus is for each of us. Let's
pause now and call to mind God's presence with us.

Sit back and get comfortable in your seat. Take a deep breath,
filling your lungs with air. / If you are comfortable doing so,
close your eyes. / Attend to the rhythm of your own breathing. /
In the quiet become aware of God's love for you. / God has
shown his love through Jesus / and wishes to continue to show
his love to you now today. / God waits for your loving response.

(Allow time for personal reflection.)

*(Ask two readers to stand and read the
Prayers of Petition on page 80.)*

A: *Open our minds, Jesus. Teach us your ways.*
You are teacher and Lord!
B: *Send us your Spirit that we may teach our
children to have faith in you.*
A: *Open our hearts, Jesus. Give us your peace.*
You heal all who come to you.
B: *Send us your Spirit that we may be a healing
presence to those who are worn down by sickness
or sadness.*
A: *Walk with us, Jesus. Be always by our side.*
You are our friend.
B: *Send us your Spirit that we may reach out to those
who are without friends, who experience
themselves as outcast. May we be their friend.*
A: *Refresh our souls, Jesus. Free us from sin.*
You are our Savior and hope!
B: *Send us your Spirit that we may bring the saving
word of God's love to those around us. May we
work with others to overcome all that oppresses the
human family.*

Send us your Spirit, God. Bless us with your wisdom. Help us
teach our children to have faith in you and to follow your Son.
We pray this in the name of Jesus, your Son,
who taught us how to live and how to love. Amen.

RESPOND

We've talked about images of Jesus presented in the Gospels and the many ways we are called to carry on the ministry of Jesus in our everyday lives. Two of the ways we can carry on this ministry are to share the teachings of Jesus with our children and to take time to deepen our own understanding of what it means to be his follower. The handouts suggest some ways of doing this.

(Refer to the handouts photocopied from pages 82–84.)

"Bringing the Message into Everyday Life" provides insight into the way each of the four Gospel writers described the person of Jesus, his life and times.

"Bringing the Message Home" presents different ways to reflect on familiar sayings of Jesus found in the Gospels. The handout also encourages you to share these passages with your children and talk about what these passages mean for us today.

"Deepening the Message" features an excerpt from an article that appeared in *U.S. Catholic* magazine. As adults, we need to live as Jesus lived and love as Jesus loved. What an amazing place this world would be if more of us did this every day!

And that concludes our session. Thank you for taking the time to be here. I hope we will see you back next time (*name the date and time*) when the topic will be "Living the Catholic Tradition."

R E A D E R   S C R I P T
Four Responses to "Who Do You Say That I Am?"

Leader: And he asked them, "But who do you say that I am?"

Reader 1: You are teacher, Jesus. When I have questions, I look to you for guidance. Your words, your stories, teach me about loving God, living with faith, and caring for others. You teach me what is important. You teach me what it means to be your follower—to live and love as you did, to reach out to those in need, to share what I have with others. You are teacher, Jesus.

Leader: And he asked them, "But who do you say that I am?"

Reader 2: You are healer, Jesus. You know my needs. You know when I am in pain. You know what needs healing in my life—sometimes before I do. You reach out to all who are suffering with compassion and love. Your presence brings healing, strength, forgiveness, and peace. You are healer, Jesus.

Leader: And he asked them, "But who do you say that I am?"

Reader 3: You are friend, walking beside me day by day. You are always there for me. You share my sorrows and my joy. When life gets rough, I turn to you. You offer comfort and support. I lean on you, Jesus. With you, I am never alone. You are friend.

Leader: And he asked them, "But who do you say that I am?"

Reader 4: You are Savior. You are the risen Christ—the resurrection and the life! You are God's Son, and through you, my sins are forgiven. Through you, I have hope. You came to set us free from all that oppresses us. You are the Savior of the world!

Leader prays: Jesus—Teacher, Healer, Friend, and Savior—be with us. Guide us as we seek to deepen our faith in you. Open our hearts to your love. Give us the courage to follow you wholeheartedly. Be with us as we journey together in faith.

Amen.

PRAYERS OF PETITION

Two Readers Petition the Lord

A: Open our minds, Jesus. Teach us your ways.
You are teacher and Lord!

B: Send us your Spirit that we may teach our children to have faith in you.

A: Open our hearts, Jesus. Gives us your peace.
You heal all who come to you.

B: Send us your Spirit that we may be a healing presence to those who are
worn down by sickness or sadness.

A: Walk with us, Jesus. Be always by our side.
You are our friend.

B: Send us your Spirit that we may reach out to those who are without
friends, who experience themselves as outcast. May we be a friend to them.

A: Refresh our souls, Jesus. Free us from sin.
You are our Savior and hope!

B: Send us your Spirit that we may bring the saving word of God's love to
those around us. May we work with others to overcome all that oppresses
the human family.

"Who Do You Say That I Am?"

"Who do you say that I am?" Two thousand years ago, Jesus asked this question of his disciples and followers. Jesus asks this same question of us today: "Who do you say that I am?"

This is the fundamental Christian question because in naming who Jesus is and how he responded to the world around him, we gain insight into who Jesus is calling us to be. At the heart of Catholic teaching is the conviction that as followers of Jesus, we are called both to know Jesus' teachings and to follow his example in our daily lives. We, too, are called to be teacher, healer, friend, and to share the saving presence of Jesus with one another. As disciples we are to follow the Master's guide—to live as Jesus lived and to love as Jesus loved.

Conversation

Now Jesus and his disciples set out for the villages of Caesarea Philippi. Along the way he asked his disciples, "Who do people say that I am?" They said in reply, "John the Baptist, others Elijah, still others one of the prophets." And he asked them, "But who do you say that I am?"

Mark 8:27–29

- ◆ Introduce yourself and talk about one insight or new idea you gained from the session.

- ◆ In the presentation, we presented four images of Jesus—Teacher, Healer, Friend, and Savior. Talk about the image that is closest to your own reflections about Jesus.

- ◆ Talk about a time when you felt you shared Jesus' presence with someone else. In what ways have you been a teacher, healer, friend, or shared the saving presence of Jesus?

- ◆ What image of Jesus does your family need to reflect on right now? What image does the parish most need to reflect on? Why?

Bringing the Message into Everyday Life

The Gospel According to . . . Matthew, Mark, Luke and John. These Gospels represent all we know about the historical Jesus. Taken together they present the life and times of Jesus as Teacher, Healer, Friend, and Savior. Individually, each Gospel provides a somewhat different "angle" on the person of Jesus.

The Gospel of Mark was written first and gave the early Christians the earliest organized account of Jesus' life and his core message of the coming of the Kingdom of God. This fast-paced Gospel gives us a picture of Jesus always on the move, usually surrounded by the crowd, and freely giving expression to his feelings of compassion, pity, and even anger.

> To get a sense of Mark's Gospel, read it all in one sitting. It gives a sweeping view of the movements of Jesus' life and the close connection between the words and actions of Jesus and his subsequent death and resurrection.

The Gospel of Matthew was written to a community made up primarily of Jewish Christians. So as the writer wove together the stories of Jesus' life and teaching, he highlighted Jesus as the promised Messiah. The writer of Matthew's Gospel makes frequent reference to events and experiences of the Jewish people and connects those with the life of Jesus.

> Read the events surrounding Jesus' birth as set out in the first two chapters. Make note of the multiple times that the words of the prophets and quotes from the Old Testament are woven into the account.

The Gospel of Luke was written about the same time as Matthew's, but is addressed to a predominantly non-Jewish community. In Luke we find a compassionate Jesus who cares for the poor and the outcast and expects his followers to do the same. For the writer of Luke's Gospel, the saving words of Jesus are intended for everyone.

> Page through Luke's Gospel and you'll find many of the best known parables, many of which are only in this Gospel. Pause along the way and read through those that appeal to you.

The Gospel of John was the last account written and is distinct from the other three. The first three accounts have much in common and are termed the Synoptic Gospels. From the opening lines of John's Gospel a different image of Jesus is shown. The manger and the Magi are gone; in their place, the writer of John's Gospel places a clear statement that Jesus is not only human but also divine.

> Chapters 14 through 16 present an image of Jesus as one who cares for his followers and will be present with them always. Take your time in reading through these chapters.

Bringing the Message Home

What words of Jesus hold special meaning for you?

Each week, reflect on a Scripture passage that highlights a teaching or saying of Jesus.

◆ Make the passage part of your daily prayer. Read the passage and then sit quietly to reflect on the meaning these words of Jesus have for you in your own life.

◆ Write the passage on a small piece of paper and place it where you will see it often during the day—on your bathroom mirror, in your car, on the refrigerator.

◆ Take time to write down your thoughts about the passage in a special notebook. Keep this notebook as a prayer journal, adding your own insights, and prayers of petition and thanks.

◆ Share this passage with your children at mealtime, while you are in the car with them, or during their prayer at night. Ask them to tell you what the passage means to them.

† Ask and it will be given to you; seek and you will find; knock and the door will be opened to you. (Mt. 7:7)

† Come to me, all you who labor and are burdened, and I will give you rest. (Mt. 11:28)

† Whoever wishes to be great among you will be your servant. (Mk. 10:43)

† You shall love the Lord your God with all your heart, with all your soul, with all your mind, and with all your strength. . . . You shall love your neighbor as yourself. (Mk. 12:30–31)

† Stop judging and you will not be judged. Stop condemning and you will not be condemned. Forgive and you will be forgiven. (Lk. 6:37)

† Give and gifts will be given to you. (Lk. 6:38)

† Jesus said to them, "I am the bread of life; whoever comes to me will never hunger, and whoever believes in me will never thirst." (John 6:35)

† I am the light of the world. Whoever follows me will not walk in darkness, but will have the light of life. (John 8:12)

† I came so that they might have life and have it more abundantly. (John 10:10)

† Peace I leave with you; my peace I give to you. (John 14:27)

Deepening the Message

"Who do you say that I am?" As Catholics, we are called to put our response to Jesus' question into action. Father Faso, the pastor of St. Peter's Church in downtown Chicago, invites us to read the Gospels in order to get close to Jesus. The Gospels provide us with a new way of seeing the world and the people around us, a way of "dreaming Gospel dreams."

Catch the Dream
By Father Charles Faso, O.F.M.

Our hungry world needs new dreams to catch its heart on fire. Our role as church, as the Body of Christ, is to be about dreaming Gospel dreams and being committed to those dreams in the world.

It is all a matter of getting close to Jesus. Saint Augustine wrote that if we do not know the Gospels, we do not know Christ—the Gospels are the place to start getting closer to the one with the dreams that can make all the difference. We all have riches and treasures deep in our pockets and purses that need to see the light of day.

We all have hungers for acceptance and affirmation, for a smile and a hug, for forgiveness and the courage to make a new start. Every hunger that each of us feels and knows too well in our own hearts and hopes, are the same hungers all men, women, and children feel and know—yes, even . . . those people who make you the most miserable or frustrated.

We, the Body of Christ, on the shores of our Sea of Galilee where we live and work, have from the Spirit of Jesus what is needed to feed all these hungers. Get close and catch the dream. Dig down deeply and grab all the love and kindness, justice and peace, hope and forgiveness that you possibly can. And then share it all with every person you meet. Whatever goodness and holiness you have, well, that will do just fine. Then the miracle can happen again and again and again.

from *U.S. Catholic,* October 1994

Living the Catholic Tradition

Why am I a Catholic? Different people have different responses. Some people may say that the long tradition of the Church, the way the teachings and rituals have existed across the ages is what they appreciate most about their Catholic faith. For others, the Church's ability to respond to contemporary issues and challenges is the reason they are Catholic. While these differences in perspective can lead to tension within the Church, there is good news within our Catholic Tradition—both a respect for the past and an eye on the future are key elements in what it means to live our lives as Catholics. We can understand these elements as "memory" and "openness." By "memory," we refer to all those elements that make up our Catholic Tradition. By "openness," we mean taking into account the experience and insights of believers today. Catholics of every age have responded to the challenges and questions of their time by balancing memory of the past with openness to the future. That is our task as well.

> So then you are no longer strangers and sojourners, but you are fellow citizens with the holy ones and members of the household of God, built upon the foundation of the apostles and prophets, with Christ Jesus himself as the capstone. Through him the whole structure is held together and grows into a temple sacred in the Lord; in him you also are being built together into a dwelling place of God in the Spirit.
>
> Ephesians 2:19–22

Leader's 3-Minute Retreat

As you prepare for this Gathering Session, pause for a moment. Take a few deep breaths and be aware of God's loving presence with you.

Prayerfully read this excerpt from Ephesians. What word or phrase speaks most clearly to you about the Church?

For Your Reflection

Sometimes we can think that the Church is changing too slowly in some areas or too quickly in others. What is your own experience of that? Which tends to be more challenging for you—being open to change in the Church or preserving Church Tradition?

Overview and Agenda

Central Theme

The strength and vitality of the Church is rooted in the ability to maintain a creative tension between memory and openness; that is, the way the Church has expressed God's revelation in the past and then puts that revelation to new expression in the present.

Objectives

This session is designed to help adults

* reflect on their understanding of the Church as a living tradition.

* recognize the way the Church builds on the past (memory) while being aware of and responding to the contemporary world (openness).

* examine their sense of the balance of memory and openness and its expression in their parish.

Schedule

	Arrival and Greetings
10 minutes	Engage
40 minutes	Explore
20 min	Presentation
20 min	Small-group conversation
10 minutes	Reflect and Respond
	Refreshments

To Do Before the Gathering Session

☐ Read the general information on planning and conducting the sessions (page 32).

☐ Identify special groups in the parish to invite to this session. Parish Council members and leaders of parish committees would find this session particularly interesting.

☐ Ask a person to read the passage from Ephesians during the Engage

section of this session. Prepare a Bible with Ephesians 2:19–22 clearly marked.

☐ Ask four people to read the parts of Paul, the Jewish leader, a young woman in her thirties, and a young person during the Explore section. (Reader Script)

☐ Set out handouts for distribution as people arrive.

Background for the Presenter

In the glossary of the *Catechism of the Catholic Church,* tradition is described as "the living transmission of the message of the Gospel in the Church." It is through the life and teaching of the Church under the guidance of the Holy Spirit that the Gospel message—ever ancient and ever new—is given expression.

The strength of Catholic teaching and practices is

the persistent presence of a healthy balance between the past and the present. The saints serve as examples of those who have worked to preserve that balance. We can honor as models of faith a second-century teacher and theologian like Irenaeus of Lyon, a 16th-century mystic like John of the Cross, and a 20th-century activist like Dorothy Day. The task of the Catholic theologian is to give

expression to the dynamic relationship between memory and openness: an awareness of our foundations as the basis for responding to contemporary settings and concerns.

Suggested reading A resource that speaks of the importance of expressing the Christian message in a way appropriate for our times is the *General Directory for Catechesis,* Part Two, Chapter I.

ENGAGE

Welcome, everyone! It is good to come together for this Gathering Session. Thank you for being with us.

What does it mean to be Catholic?

During the next hour, we're going to take some time to explore what it means to live our lives as Catholics. We'll talk about some of the traditions and teachings of the Church that guide us and challenge us in the way we live our lives. We'll also talk about how our own experiences and the situations we face—in our families, in our places of work, in our community, and in our world—bring deeper understanding and insight to our Catholic teachings and traditions.

As Catholics, we hold core beliefs in common, and yet we also have remarkably different experiences of what it means to be Catholic. That's where we want to begin our conversation: What does it mean to be Catholic? Each person here may have a different response. Think about it for a moment: How would you respond if someone asked you, "Why are you Catholic? What is something you appreciate most about your Catholic faith?"

(Allow time for personal reflection.)

Keep that response in your thoughts.

Some things people appreciate about the Catholic faith

What is it people appreciate most about their Catholic faith? Some people might say that going to Mass on Sunday is the most important part of their Catholic faith. For others, belonging to a parish, being involved, and feeling welcomed is what they appreciate most. Some would say that a strong devotion to Mary or our Catholic Tradition of the Communion of Saints holds great significance for them. Others find that Catholic social teaching—being involved in service, working for justice—is what makes their Catholic faith most meaningful.

Why be Catholic? You might find it interesting to know how the person sitting next to you would respond to that question.

I invite you to turn to a person near you. Introduce yourselves. Then tell each other how you would respond.

"Why are you Catholic—What is it that you appreciate most about your Catholic faith?"

(Allow time for participants to talk to one another. When you feel they have had time to share their responses, you may ask if anyone wishes to share their response with the larger group. Then move on to the opening prayer.)

Thank you. We listen now to a reading from the Letter of Paul to the Ephesians:

(Have a reader come forward to proclaim Ephesians 2:19–22, using a Bible. Having quiet music playing in the background enhances the reflective tone.)

Reading: Ephesians 2:19–22

So then you are no longer strangers and sojourners, but you are fellow citizens with the holy ones and members of the household of God, built upon the foundation of the apostles and prophets, with Christ Jesus himself as the capstone. Through him the whole structure is held together and grows into a temple sacred in the Lord; in him you also are being built together into a dwelling place of God in the Spirit.

The Word of the Lord.

Response: Thanks be to God.

Leader: Let us pray . . .

Loving God,
We come together in a spirit of faith:
Each of us with different experiences and stories,
Each of us with different insights and questions.
Be with us as we explore the meaning of our faith.
Open us to the insights of others.
Help us listen to your voice within our own hearts.
Send us your Spirit as we seek to deepen our faith.
Bless us with the wisdom and love we need to pass this faith on to our children.
We pray this in the name of Jesus, who is our foundation and strength, whose love unites us all.
Amen.

(Substitute "the children" or "this parish" for "our children" as appropriate.)

EXPLORE

Elements of
the Church that are of
significance to people:

What does it mean to be Catholic? What, for you, is the most important dimension of being Catholic? The responses to these questions are as numerous and varied as the number of people present here now.

. . . Church practices, prayers, and teaching

Some people find the traditions of the Church most important and meaningful to them. Perhaps it's the familiar rhythm of the Sunday liturgy or the place of devotions to Mary. The consistency of the Church's prayer and ritual over the years and the clarity of Catholic teaching: these traditions are important for them.

. . . The Second Vatican Council and Catholic social teaching

Others, however, find their reasons for being Catholic connected with the Church's vision of the future. This vision for the future is reflected in the writings of The Second Vatican Council, which challenged the Church to "read the signs of the times." The Church looks to the future when it works to overcome the effects of oppression, or when it strives to address the social and ethical issues facing people today.

This variety can also lead to tension.

Remembering the traditions of the past or being open to the future—people can easily disagree on what is more important to our Catholic faith, and these different points of view can often lead to tension within the Church, even within a parish community.

Tension addressed in Catholic respect for the past with an eye toward the future

But there is good news within our Catholic tradition—both a respect for the past and an eye on the future are key elements in what it means to live our lives as Catholics. We can understand these elements as "memory" and "openness." By "memory," we refer to all those elements that make up our Catholic Tradition. By "openness," we mean taking into account the experiences and insights of believers today.

This desire to keep memory and openness in balance is distinctively Catholic and is one of a number of distinguishing elements of our Catholic tradition—one that we would want to hand on to others.

Memory as a link to the past

We are a Church rooted in a long and solid tradition. The reading from Paul's letter to the Ephesians makes that clear when it says that we are part of the household of God "built upon the foundation of the apostles and prophets, with Christ Jesus himself as the capstone."

We are a people rooted in the firm foundation of the past, a people who value and depend upon memory.

Openness as an approach to the future

On the other hand, the Church exists not as a past, complete reality but as a living, breathing entity located in a specific time and place. As Paul writes in his letter to the Ephesians, "in [the Lord] you also are being built together into a dwelling place of God in the Spirit."

In addition to being a people who value and depend upon memory, we are also a people drawn to the future, guided by the Holy Spirit with a lively sense of openness.

The relationship between memory and openness is not new; the Church has been working to maintain this balance from the very beginning.

Early debate concerning the need for Gentile Christians to follow Jewish laws and customs

If we go back to the early years of the Church, we can see one of the first situations that caused tension between memory and openness. Most of the early Christians were Jewish; they were raised Jewish, they followed Jewish laws and teachings. But they also believed that Jesus, a Jew, was their Messiah. For them, being Jewish and being Christian wasn't a conflict but a natural movement.

The problem came up when Gentiles—those who were not Jewish—wanted to follow Jesus, wanted to become Christian. It seemed clear to some Jewish Christians that the Gentiles should first agree to follow Jewish law. That was the way to preserve their Jewish traditions while following the teachings of Jesus.

Others in the early Church, the apostle Paul in particular, disagreed. Paul said it was enough to believe in Jesus Christ. Jesus is the source of our salvation. This difference in opinion caused a major tension between memory of the past and openness to the future.

Let's take a moment to imagine what the debate in the early Church might have sounded like . . . we'll let Paul speak first.

(Ask the reader speaking as Paul to stand and read from the Reader Script.)

— 🕊 —

Reader 1:
(as Saint Paul)

I believe—no, I know—that God has called me to proclaim the Good News of Jesus Christ to the Gentiles. This is my calling. And I also believe—in fact, I know—that Jesus is all we need. Following Jewish laws, eating some things and not others, is not as important as believing in Jesus. This all makes sense to me and to many others, but some of the

Jewish Christians refuse to accept people who don't follow Jewish laws.

Many of the leaders in the Jewish Christian community refuse to sit down and eat with Christian Gentiles because they are afraid of violating Jewish law by eating with people who are considered unclean. I understand that they are saying this because of Jewish laws and traditions created in the past. But we must also be open to the future.

I am trying to ask you to see beyond the laws! It is not necessary to circumcise the Gentiles and direct them to observe the Law of Moses. What is important is that they accept Christ. It is Christ who unites us now. I am begging you to accept the Gentile believers so that I can continue to do my work—to spread the Good News of Christ to everyone who wants to hear it!

— 🕊 —

Leader: Paul's emphasis was on being open to the spread of the Gospel to all people. If this meant setting aside some past practices or ways of thinking, so be it.

But not everyone agreed. Some maintained that it was the memory of their own past that should be given priority. Here is a point of view from one of the Jews who had recently become Christian in the early Church.

(Ask the reader representing a first-century Jewish Christian to stand and read from the Reader Script.)

— 🕊 —

Reader 2:
(as first-century
Jewish Christian)

It seems the tension and the disagreements will never settle down. Before the so-called apostle Paul came along, everything was going fine: we were good Jews who followed the ancient traditions of the Jewish faith and accepted the teachings of Jesus Christ. And that's the way it should be; that's the way it has always been. After all, Jesus was a Jew; he followed Jewish law.

The problem started when that apostle, Paul, began saying that Jesus came to save everyone. That's fair enough. But then Paul said that the Gentiles didn't have to follow Jewish law and the men didn't have to be circumcised. Now, I believe that if Gentiles— people outside the Jewish faith—want to become Christian, that's fine. But they must first commit themselves to honor Jewish traditions and the laws set out by Moses. Men must be circumcised. All Gentiles who wish to be Christian must follow Jewish dietary rules. That only makes sense, and that's the way we have been doing it from the beginning. We have followed these laws all our life. We must preserve our traditions and ways. Surely God does not want us to change the law!

— ✍ —

Leader: At one level, this debate was resolved at the Council of Jerusalem in about 50 A.D., some 20 years after the life, death, and resurrection of Jesus. But the relationship between our Jewish heritage and our openness to a new way of understanding our relationship with God continued across the history of the Church and is present even today.

The history of the Church is marked by these experiences of tension between memory and openness. At times when parts of the Church resisted the changes in the world around them or attempted to narrow the message of Jesus, limiting the scope of the Good News, there were always people who challenged this and pointed with hope to the future.

At other times when elements of the Church were forgetting our shared heritage and becoming too comfortable with the culture around them or with the power they held, there were people who called them—called us—to look with faith to a memory of what is truly at the heart of our Tradition.

Interestingly, some of those people who have reminded us of our Tradition or have called us to new openness are numbered among the saints.

The example of
St. Francis of Assisi   Saint Francis of Assisi is a good example. Francis called the Church to remember its traditions at a time when many in the Church were forgetting what was core to our faith. The late 1100s and early 1200s were a challenging time in the Church. A number of heresies, or false teachings, were making inroads among Church members. Many people in the Church responded sharply and harshly to those who held these false teachings, punishing them with torture and even death. This was the period of the Inquisition, one of the most negative periods in our Church's history.

But some people, like Francis, saw that the solution to this issue was not punishing those with false beliefs, but calling all Christians back to the core message of the Gospel. Through his voluntary poverty and the example of his community's life, Francis and those who followed him called the Church back to its best memory—the simple message of God's love.

The apostle Paul and the Jewish Christian leaders, Saint Francis, and countless others have worked and prayed and relied on the guidance of the Holy Spirit to maintain the balance between memory of our tradition and openness to our future. And that is our task today—to continue to live within the wonderful tension of memory and openness.

Application to the present

In the past when we thought about the foundations of what it means to be Catholic, we might have made reference to external expressions, such as membership in a particular parish, attendance at Sunday Mass, or devotion to the saints. And while these are important, they are expressions of a larger reality.

Foundation for being Catholic rooted more in world view than in particular action

What serves as the foundation of being Catholic, what we want to hand on to future generations, includes not only the external expressions but the perspective we have on our faith and on the world.

One of these perspectives is the "both/and" nature of the Catholic response to the world. We are a people not only of memory nor exclusively of openness. We live in the tension between these two realities . . . a challenging but exciting place to live.

And each of us lives in that tension in a somewhat different way. On any given issue, we each would tend to emphasize memory over openness *or* openness over memory.

Across history, the Church has sometimes emphasized one over the other.

Across our history as a Church, we have at various times placed more emphasis on memory than might be helpful for the Church into the future *or* been so open as to forget the heart of who we are rooted in our tradition.

To live in that tension is at the heart of what it means to be an engaged member of the Catholic Church.

So what about us?

So what does that look like for us today? How does this shape our response to what it means to be a Catholic today?

Let me propose three perspectives that connect this notion of the balancing of memory and openness to our own lives as Catholics.

**Perspective 1:
Looking at some of the tensions in the Church in light of memory and openness**

First, it is possible and even helpful to view some of the tensions in the Church today—and perhaps even in this parish—in light of the relationship between memory and openness.

It is easy sometimes to use labels such as "conservative" and "liberal" to describe those with whom we disagree. And these labels make it easier to dismiss someone's perspectives or beliefs. "She is so conservative." "He is too liberal."

What if we think of one another not in terms of liberal and conservative, but in terms of memory and openness? "She is attentive to the memory of our tradition." "He is open to the future."

Examples of the dynamics of memory and openness

Here is an example. A woman in her early thirties speaks in this way of her understanding of the Church.

(Ask the reader representing the woman to stand and read from the Reader Script.)

Reader 3:
(a woman in her early thirties)

I was baptized a Catholic, but my parents didn't go to church very much. My grandmother is the one who taught me what little I know about my Catholic faith. Whenever I stayed with her, we would go to church on Sunday. I loved the candles and the incense and the hymns. At her house, she read stories to me from the Bible. But my grandmother lived in a different town, and I didn't get to see her very often. Now I have young children of my own, and I want them to have what I didn't have when I was growing up. I want them to know the traditions of the Catholic Church. I want us to go to Mass every Sunday. I want my children to learn about what the Church teaches. Some people think the Church should be more open to change. And that may be so. But I think it is the traditions of the Church that give us stability. And that stability is what we need to face the challenges in our changing world.

Participation in liturgy, attention to the teachings of the Church, valuing the stability of the Church over its openness to change: this mom's comments reflect an awareness of and an appreciation for the memory of the Church.

In the same parish, we might hear this from another young person:

(Ask the reader representing a young person to stand and read from the Reader Script.)

— 🕊 —

Reader 4:
(a young person)

I grew up Catholic and was involved in almost everything you can be involved in at church. I sang with the choir, joined the youth group, participated in prayer and Bible studies, went on service trips. But as I grow older, I feel more and more frustrated. I wish the Church were more open to change. Sometimes the teachings and traditions of the Church seem so out of touch with our problems today. Why is it that so many in the Church seem to fear change? I think that change helps keep our faith fresh and alive. If the Church is going to be meaningful in people's lives and make a difference in the world around us, it is going to have to be more open to change.

— 🕊 —

Leader:

Our Church needs both memory, which holds firmly to the past, and openness that allows us to move into the future. As we look at the Church in the present and into the future, we recognize that we have new questions, new experiences, and new perspectives that the Church has never had to deal with before. Memory provides a solid framework for responding to these questions. But without openness to the experiences and the insights of believers today, that memory can become static and dead.

Perspective 2:
No one group has the whole answer to what it means to be Catholic.

Second, whether we tend to emphasize memory or openness, it seems important to recognize that no one person, no one group has the whole picture to what it means to be Catholic. Over the centuries, the Catholic Church has survived and thrived at the intersection of memory and openness. While each of us brings our own perspective to the realities of the present Church, acknowledging and affirming the need for complementary and even conflicting points of view is key to what it means to be Catholic and to contribute to the ongoing vibrancy of the Church.

Perspective 3:
Fostering a willingness to engage in conversation with those who differ from us

And finally, as we look to the future of the Church, whether from the perspective of memory or openness, it is important that we foster in ourselves and in future generations a willingness to engage in conversation with those whose perspectives differ from ours. As we look back at our history as a Church, both recent and distant, we can see that the Church has been most vital and most influential when its most diverse and sometimes divergent voices have been heard.

(Small-group conversation)

Genuinely listening to the position of others and carefully giving expression to our own: these are essential to the ongoing life and growth of the Church. Let's put them into practice now as we move into small-group conversation.

(Invite participants to form groups of 6 or 7, including a facilitator. Explain that the groups will have 15 minutes for conversation on the points outlined on the handout.)

(As the time for small-group conversation comes to a close, invite the participants to bring their attention back to the full group. Invite the small-group facilitators to share insights from their groups.)

REFLECT

*(Instrumental music playing softly in the background
enhances the sense of prayerfulness.)*

(Pause briefly at each / mark.)

As our time together comes to a close, let's take a moment to
quiet ourselves and rest in God's presence.

Sit back and get comfortable in your seat. Take a deep breath,
filling your lungs with air. / If you are comfortable doing so,
close your eyes. / Attend to the rhythm of your own breathing. /
As you breathe in, remember that it is the Spirit of God that
dwells within you. / As you breathe out, remember that that
same presence is in our Church and in the world. / The Holy
Spirit is the sign of God's great love for you. / God waits for
your loving response.

(Allow time for personal reflection.)

(Pray each line slowly with brief pauses.)

Loving God,
You have blessed our Church with memories of rich
    traditions and history.
You have sent your Holy Spirit to help us be open to
    changing needs and times.
Be with us now.
Give us wisdom to know how to carry on the holy
    traditions of our Church.
Grace us with strength to change what needs to be
    changed.
Make us instruments of peace, not division.
Open our ears to listen.
Open our eyes to see the goodness in others.
Open our hearts to understand.
Make of us a compassionate, wise, and holy people.
We pray this in the name of Jesus your Son,
Amen.

RESPOND

Throughout history, Catholics have responded to the challenges of their time by balancing memory of the Church's past traditions with openness to the future. Two pages of your handouts offer ways for us to work toward achieving this balance.

(Refer to the handouts photocopied from pages 104–106.)

"Bringing the Message into Everyday Life" features seven principles to help people with different points of view talk about important issues. As adults, we need to use these principles to help us engage in important conversations in the Church today.

"Bringing the Message Home" offers a mini-retreat for your family. The retreat takes place within the setting of a family meal and provides a creative way for you to talk with your children about faith and traditions and values that you hope to pass on to them.

"Deepening the Message" is a discussion of the Communion of Saints for your personal reflection.

And that concludes our session. Thank you for taking the time to be here. I hope we will see you back next time (*name the date and time*) when we will look at the role of liturgy, particularly the Eucharist, in our lives together as Catholics.

(Leader asks Reader 1 to read.)

Reader 1:
(as Saint Paul)
I believe—no, I know—that God has called me to proclaim the Good News of Jesus Christ to the Gentiles. This is my calling. And I also believe—in fact, I know—that Jesus is all we need. Following Jewish laws, eating some things and not others, is not as important as believing in Jesus. This all makes sense to me and to many others, but some of the Jewish Christians refuse to accept people who don't follow Jewish laws.

Many of the leaders in the Jewish Christian community refuse to sit down and eat with Christian Gentiles because they are afraid of violating Jewish law by eating with people who are considered unclean. I understand that they are saying this because of Jewish laws and traditions created in the past. But we must also be open to the future.

I am trying to ask you to see beyond the laws! It is not necessary to circumcise the Gentiles and direct them to observe the Law of Moses. What is important is that they accept Christ. It is Christ who unites us now. I am begging you to accept the Gentile believers so that I can continue to do my work—to spread the Good News of Christ to everyone who wants to hear it!

READER SCRIPT

Reflections on Memory: A First-Century Jewish Christian

(Leader asks Reader 2 to read.)

Reader 2:
(as first-century
Jewish Christian)

It seems the tension and the disagreements will never settle down. Before the so-called apostle Paul came along, everything was going fine: we were good Jews who followed the ancient traditions of the Jewish faith and accepted the teachings of Jesus Christ. And that's the way it should be; that's the way it has always been. After all, Jesus was a Jew; he followed Jewish law.

The problem started when that apostle, Paul, began saying that Jesus came to save everyone. That's fair enough. But then Paul said that the Gentiles didn't have to follow Jewish law and the men didn't have to be circumcised. Now, I believe that if Gentiles—people outside the Jewish faith—want to become Christian, that's fine. But they must first commit themselves to honor Jewish traditions and the laws set out by Moses. Men must be circumcised. All Gentiles who wish to be Christian must follow Jewish dietary rules. That only makes sense, and that's the way we have been doing it from the beginning. We have followed these laws all our life. We must preserve our traditions and ways. Surely God does not want us to change the law!

(Leader asks Reader 3 to read.)

Reader 3:
(as a woman in her early thirties)

I was baptized a Catholic, but my parents didn't go to church very much. My grandmother is the one who taught me what little I know about my Catholic faith. Whenever I stayed with her, we would go to church on Sunday. I loved the candles and the incense and the hymns. At her house, she read stories to me from the Bible. But my grandmother lived in a different town, and I didn't get to see her very often. Now I have young children of my own, and I want them to have what I didn't have when I was growing up. I want them to know the traditions of the Catholic Church. I want us to go to Mass every Sunday. I want my children to learn about what the Church teaches. Some people think the Church should be more open to change. And that may be so. But I think it is the traditions of the Church that give us stability. And that stability is what we need to face the challenges in our changing world.

READER SCRIPT

Reflections on Openness: A Contemporary Young Person

(Leader asks Reader 4 to read.)

Reader 4:
(as a young person)

I grew up Catholic and was involved in almost everything you can be involved in at church. I sang with the choir, joined the youth group, participated in prayer and Bible studies, went on service trips. But as I grow older, I feel more and more frustrated. I wish the Church were more open to change. Sometimes the teachings and traditions of the Church seem so out of touch with our problems today. Why is it that so many in the Church seem to fear change? I think that change helps keep our faith fresh and alive. If the Church is going to be meaningful in people's lives and make a difference in the world around us, it is going to have to be more open to change.

Living the Catholic Tradition

Why am I a Catholic? Different people have different responses. Some people may say that the long tradition of the Church, the way the teachings and rituals have existed across the ages is what they appreciate most about their Catholic faith. For others, the Church's ability to respond to contemporary issues and challenges is the reason they are Catholic. While these differences in perspective can lead to tension within the Church, there is good news within our Catholic Tradition—both a respect for the past and an eye on the future are key elements in what it means to live our lives as Catholics. We can understand these elements as "memory" and "openness." By "memory," we refer to all those elements that make up our Catholic Tradition. By "openness," we mean taking into account the experience and insights of believers today. Catholics of every age have responded to the challenges and questions of their time by balancing memory of the past with openness to the future. That is our task as well.

Conversation

Think about these things:

Some of the most important Catholic traditions that should be passed onto our children are

_____

_____

Something I deeply appreciate about my Catholic faith is

_____

_____

If I were to make a television commercial for the Catholic Church, I would be sure to include

_____

_____

- ◆ Introduce yourself and talk about one insight or new idea you gained from the session.

- ◆ Talk about a situation today in which you think the Church needs to be more aware of being open to change.

or

Talk about a situation in which you think the Church needs to pay more attention to its traditions.

- ◆ Which tends to be more challenging for you—being open to change in the Church or preserving Church Tradition?

Session C — *Living the Catholic Tradition*

Handout C1

Bringing the Message into Everyday Life

Common Ground is an initiative launched by Cardinal Joseph Bernardin in 1996. His vision was to create a "common ground" for liberal, moderate, and conservative Catholics to address issues vital to the life of the Catholic Church in the United States. The Common Ground project offers seven principles of dialogue to help people with different points of view talk about issues together without the distrust and polarization that often leads to argument. Try using these principles of dialogue in parish meetings and discussions.

Common Ground: Principles of Dialogue

1. We should recognize that no single group or viewpoint in the Church has a complete monopoly on the truth. Solutions to the Church's problems will almost inevitably emerge from a variety of sources.

2. No group within the Church should judge itself alone to be possessed of enlightenment.

3. We should test all proposals for their usefulness in supporting people in living Christian lives as well as for their theological truth.

4. We should presume that those with whom we differ are acting in good faith. They deserve civility, charity, and a good-faith effort to understand their concerns. We should not use labels, or blanketing terms such as "radical feminism," "the hierarchy," "the Vatican" for living, complicated realities.

5. We should put the best possible construction on differing positions, addressing their strongest points rather than seizing upon the most vulnerable aspects in order to discredit them.

6. We should be cautious in ascribing motives. We should not impugn another's love of the Church and loyalty to it.

7. We should bring the Church to engage the realities of contemporary culture by acknowledging both our culture's valid achievements and real dangers.

Ultimately, the fresh eyes and changed hearts we need cannot be distilled from guidelines. They emerge in the space created by praise and worship. The revitalized Catholic common ground will be marked by a determined pastoral effort to keep the liturgy, above all, from becoming a battleground for confrontation and polarization, and to treasure it as the common worship of God through Jesus Christ in the communion of the Holy Spirit.

To read the entire text of the Principles of Dialogue and to learn more about the Common Ground project, go to www.nplc.org/commonground.htm.

© Loyola Press

Bringing the Message Home

How do we pass our faith onto our children? One of the best ways for parents to pass on their faith to their children is to take time to talk about it. But sometimes, it is hard to know how to make time for these kinds of conversations! Here is a simple suggestion for a mini-retreat for you and your family to enjoy together— a time for you to talk about your faith, to share your ideas and values, and to celebrate the love you have for each other. Read over the retreat; adapt it to fit your style. And then take time to do it.

Sharing Faith at Mealtime

Select a time when your family can all sit down together for a meal. Have your children help you plan the menu. Nothing elaborate, but simple foods that you will all enjoy. When you are about to eat, light a candle on the table, take the phone off the hook, and begin with a prayer of grace, asking God to bless the food and your time together.

Set two bowls on the table. Write out questions or statements on small slips of paper. (Use the "conversation starters" below to give you ideas and add some of your own.) Place the conversation starters for parents/adults in one bowl and the ones for children in another. During the meal, invite each person at the table to take a slip of paper out of a bowl and respond to the statement or question. Here are some ideas to get you started.

Conversation Starters for Parents/Adults

- Tell a story about a person who has taught you about your faith. What did you learn from this person?
- Talk about something you appreciate or value about your Catholic faith.
- What is your favorite prayer? When and where do you pray it?

End with this simple prayer of thanks:

Conversation Starters for Children

- Tell about one of your favorite stories about Jesus. Why do you like this story?
- Name a place where you feel close to Jesus.
- Name a place you like to go to pray.
- Tell about a person you know who shows Jesus' love to others.

Loving God, thank you for the gift of being together as a family.
Help us show our love for one another.
Fill our hearts with your kindness and love. Amen.

© Loyola Press

Deepening the Message

One of the elements of the Catholic Tradition that helps us in our task of balancing memory and openness is the Church's teaching on the Communion of Saints. The saints provide examples for us of the variety of ways in which people have lived out the faith in different times and settings.

May the Circle Be Unbroken: Why Catholics Treasure Their Saints
By Elizabeth Johnson, C.S.J., and Kathy Coffey

The church is a community of shared life in Jesus, wherein everyone is called to holiness. In this community, as in all human life, no one is a solitary player, but everyone depends on everyone else and is affected for better or worse by what others do or omit to do. When anyone responds to the gift of grace, the shape of his or her life becomes an influence that strengthens faith for others.

In this community, saints function like sacraments. They are examples of the different ways discipleship can be lived, some even having taken successful risks to forge new paths of holiness in new cultural settings. Most of all, they are signs of hope, living pledges of the divine promise of the future, showing us that the struggle for love and justice is worth it. Their prayers for the church strengthen us all in faith.

In response, the living church honors the saints by loving these friends of Christ and cherishing their memory— as Vatican II puts it. This is done when we tell their stories; when we thank God for them; when we take a clue from their example for our own pattern of life; when in the midst of suffering and oppression, we allow the act of remembrance to unleash our energies for justice; when we call upon them as partners in the struggle.

Active belief in the communion of saints is a movement of hope in God, who raises the dead to life and promises a future to all the dead, to our loved ones, even to us.

from *U.S. Catholic,* November 1994

Invitation to the Feast

The documents of the Second Vatican Council remind us that the liturgy is the "summit" toward which the life of the Church is directed and the "font" from which the Church's power flows. But for many people, going to Mass on Sunday is simply an obligation, something to squeeze into a busy weekend or to set aside if the day is too hectic. However, if we consider the liturgy not as an obligation, but rather as an invitation, our perspective might change. The liturgy is an invitation to participate in the life of God. The invitation is present in the words of Scripture, in the gathered assembly, and in the consecrated bread and wine. As we enter into the Sunday liturgy with more attention and care, we can recognize God's invitation and the importance it can have for our lives.

Leader's 3-Minute Retreat

As you begin to prepare for this Gathering Session, pause for a moment and be aware of God's loving presence with you.

Prayerfully read this parable from Luke's Gospel. What might those who are giving excuses feel as they see the servant approaching?

Imagine yourself to be the servant who must follow the master's commands. What is your reaction to the events of the parable?

For Your Reflection

Too often Sunday liturgy can become just another thing to do. At times, our presence is only halfhearted, and we are easily distracted by other concerns.

Reflect on ways you can enhance your own participation in Sunday Mass.

"A man gave a great dinner to which he invited many. When the time for the dinner came, he dispatched his servant to say to those invited, 'Come, everything is now ready.' But one by one, they all began to excuse themselves. The first said to him, 'I have purchased a field and must go to examine it; I ask you, consider me excused.' And another said, 'I have purchased five yoke of oxen and am on my way to evaluate them; I ask you, consider me excused.' And another said, 'I have just married a woman, and therefore I cannot come.' The servant went and reported this to his master. Then the master of the house in a rage commanded his servant, 'Go out quickly into the streets and alleys of the town and bring in here the poor and the crippled, the blind and the lame.' The servant reported, 'Sir, your orders have been carried out and still there is room.' The master then ordered the servant, 'Go out to the highways and hedgerows and make people come in that my home may be filled.'"

Luke 14:16–23

Overview and Agenda

Central Theme

The liturgy embodies the invitation-response dynamics of God's relationship with human beings. In the liturgy we are invited to participate in God's presence in Word and Sacrament.

Objectives

This session is designed to
- provide an opportunity for adults to reflect on their understanding of liturgy with a particular focus on the Eucharist.
- highlight the way the Eucharist reflects the invitation-response dynamic that is at the heart of Catholic theology.
- discuss ways in which the participants can more fully experience Sunday liturgy.

Schedule

	Arrival and Greetings
10 minutes	Engage
40 minutes	Explore
20 min	Presentation
20 min	Small-group conversation
10 minutes	Reflect and Respond
	Refreshments

To Do Before the Gathering Session

- ☐ Read the general information on planning and conducting the sessions (page 32).

- ☐ Identify special groups in the parish to invite to this session. Inviting liturgical ministers, parents of children preparing for first Eucharist, and participants in the RCIA would be appropriate.

- ☐ Arrange for someone to read the passage from Luke during the Engage portion of this session. Prepare a Bible with Luke 14:16–23 clearly marked.

- ☐ Arrange to have three people serve as readers for the Explore section (each person will read two brief reflections). Choose readers appropriate to the passages on the Reader Script. Photocopy the appropriate pages and give them to the readers prior to the session.

- ☐ Set out handouts for distribution as people arrive.

Background for the Presenter

The Constitution on the Sacred Liturgy, the first of the documents from the Second Vatican Council to be approved (December 1963), serves as a rich resource for exploring the centrality of Eucharist to the Catholic life.

"Nevertheless the liturgy is the summit toward which the activity of the Church is directed; at the same time it is the font from which all her power flows." (CSL 10)

"The Church earnestly desires that all the faithful should be led to that fully conscious, and active participation in liturgical celebrations which is demanded by the very nature of the liturgy. Such participation by the Christian people . . . is their right and duty by reason of their baptism." (CSL 14)

Suggested reading A resource for exploring the Constitution on the Sacred Liturgy in conversation with a faith formation committee or a liturgy committee is *Vatican II in Plain English: The Constitutions* by Bill Huebsch with Paul Thrumes. It provides a paraphrase of the text and a process for studying the text that helps make the connection between faith and life. (Thomas More, 1997)

See also the *Catechism of the Catholic Church*, particularly #1076–1109.

ENGAGE

Welcome, everyone! It is good to come together for this Gathering Session. Thank you for being with us.

Importance of liturgy as source of Christian life

During our time together, we're going to explore what the Sunday liturgy means to us as we live our lives as Catholics. The Second Vatican Council described the Mass as the most important source of our "true Christian Spirit." But what role does the Sunday liturgy really play in our lives?

Sunday Mass is important but . . .

All of us know that the Mass is important, and yet, when was the last time you—or one of your children—got up early on a Sunday morning and said, "Wow! I can hardly wait to get to church!" Have you ever heard a friend say to you, "I don't think I could make it through the week without the Sunday liturgy. I have to be at Mass on Sunday!"

Attitudes toward liturgy

Just why is it that we get up and go to Mass? Who invites us to celebrate? Why is the Mass so important to us? These are the questions that shape our time together.

As we begin, I'd like you to take a moment to think about your response to three different statements. In your mind, decide if you agree or disagree. On a scale of 1 to 5 with "1" meaning you strongly agree and "5" meaning you strongly disagree, where are you?

Statement 1

Statement 1: The Sunday liturgy is an important part of my life.
Do you agree or disagree?

Statement 2

Statement 2: I want my children's appreciation of and participation in the Liturgy to be the same as mine.
Do you agree or disagree?

Statement 3

Statement 3: I spend Sundays differently than I do the other days of the week.
Do you agree or disagree?

I invite you to turn to a person next to you and talk about your response to one of these three statements—perhaps the one you felt most strongly about.

(Read the three statements again and then allow participants to talk to one another. After about three minutes, you may ask if anyone wishes to share their response with the larger group. Then move on to the reading from Scripture.)

Now let us quiet ourselves as we prepare to listen to a familiar parable from the Gospel of Luke.

(The reader comes forward with a Bible and proclaims the parable, Luke 14:16–23.)

— 📖 —

Reading: Luke 14:16–23

"A man gave a great dinner to which he invited many. When the time for the dinner came, he dispatched his servant to say to those invited, 'Come, everything is now ready.' But one by one, they all began to excuse themselves. The first said to him, 'I have purchased a field and must go to examine it; I ask you, consider me excused.' And another said, 'I have purchased five yoke of oxen and am on my way to evaluate them; I ask you, consider me excused.' And another said, 'I have just married a woman, and therefore I cannot come.' The servant went and reported this to his master. Then the master of the house in a rage commanded his servant, 'Go out quickly into the streets and alleys of the town and bring in here the poor and the crippled, the blind and the lame.' The servant reported, 'Sir, your orders have been carried out and still there is room.' The master then ordered the servant, 'Go out to the highways and hedgerows and make people come in that my home may be filled.'"

The Gospel of the Lord.

— 📖 —

Response: Praise to you, Lord Jesus Christ.

Leader: We listen to your Word with a spirit of faith.
You invite us to your banquet . . . Let us hear your
    invitation!
You invite us to be with you . . . Let us not refuse!
You invite us to your feast . . . Let us respond with joy!
Loving God,
Open our hearts to your invitation.
Be with us as we explore the meaning of our faith.
May your love inspire us to deepen our relationship with
    you and with one another.
We pray this in the name of Jesus, whose love unites us all.
Amen.

EXPLORE

Who would turn down an invitation to a great banquet? The food was ready. Anybody who was anybody was going to be there. It was going to be a terrific party with great music and fine wine.

Why did people turn down the invitation to the banquet?

The guests in Luke's Gospel had already said they would come. When they first received the invitation, they replied, "Yes, of course I'm coming!" and they penciled the date in on their calendars. But suddenly, that invitation was set aside by the demands of life. These are busy people!

The excuses given

We might wonder about their excuses—why the land needed to be checked on the same day as the banquet rather than later in the week; or why the oxen need to be looked at that exact moment. There probably were some good reasons for the excuses. Maybe the newly married couple had non-refundable tickets for their honeymoon, and they were going to be out of town. We don't know.

From invitation to obligation

But somewhere along the way the invitation to the banquet had become more like an obligation—one of many things that the guests were supposed to do. As one of many obligations, going to the banquet could easily be set aside in favor of an obligation that seemed more pressing, more important.

"I ask you, consider me excused."

And so the guests responded to the invitation by speaking of other obligations that had taken priority, and each of them concluded with "I ask you, consider me excused."

Sunday liturgy—invitation or obligation?

Invitation. Obligation. It seems that we view events quite differently based on whether we see them as invitation or as obligation. And that is the lens we're going to use today to explore the Mass. Do we think of Sunday liturgy as obligation or invitation?

If we are honest, going to Mass on Sunday often seems like obligation—one more thing we need to try to do in an already busy weekend.

Reflect back to the parable and consider what excuses we might offer if that parable was told today:

(Read the following excerpts of the biblical parable.)

Reading: Luke 14:17–20

"When the time for the dinner came, he dispatched his servant to say to those invited, 'Come, everything is now ready.' But one by one, they all began to excuse themselves.

The first said to him, 'I have purchased a field and must go to examine it; I ask you, consider me excused.'"

Now let's listen to some present-day excuses.

(Ask reader representing a working single mom to stand and read from the first Reader Script.)

— 🕊 —

Reader 1:
(a working single mom)

I am just starting to make some real advances in my job at work. That's important because I'm a single parent, and we depend completely on my salary. On Sunday morning, I get up early while the kids are still sleeping to try to catch up on reports. Then I work on the house, do the laundry, and help the kids with their homework. Before I know it, it's time to go to bed. Sunday is just one more crazy day in the week. Mass? I ask you, consider me excused!

— 🕊 —

Leader:
"And another said, 'I have purchased five yoke of oxen and am on my way to evaluate them; I ask you, consider me excused.'"

(Ask reader representing a busy father to stand and read from the first Reader Script.)

— 🕊 —

Reader 2:
(busy father of a young family)

I know going to Mass on Sunday is important. I always get something out of it when I go. But it's just so hard to get there. The boys have soccer practice on Sunday morning. Sometimes we travel to games. With both of us working, my wife and I are always scrambling on the weekends to get everything done. When we"re home, sometimes we just sleep in. We're exhausted. Sunday Mass? I ask you, consider me excused!

— 🕊 —

Leader:
"And another said, 'I have just married a woman, and therefore I cannot come.'"

(Ask reader representing a middle-aged woman to stand and read from the first Reader Script.)

Reader 3:
(a middle-aged woman with aging parents)

Both of my parents are really starting to show their age. I think my dad is in the beginning stages of Alzheimer's. I worry about them. So every weekend, I go to their house to check on them, make sure there's enough food, and that things are relatively clean. They only live an hour away, but I like to drive there on Sunday mornings when traffic isn't so bad. Go to Mass? Consider me excused!

Leader:

For these people—and perhaps for many of us—Sunday liturgy has become an obligation. In fact, we often speak about going to Mass as doing our "Sunday obligation."

But in fact, the liturgy in its essence and in its celebration is primarily invitation.

Liturgy as God's invitation to us

What does that mean? The liturgy in its essence—that is, in its core meaning—is God's invitation to us to be in relationship with God and with one another through Jesus.

The writers of the *Catechism of the Catholic Church* express it this way:

Quote: CCC 1082

In the Church's liturgy the divine blessing is fully revealed and communicated. The Father is acknowledged and adored as the source and the end of all the blessings of creation and salvation. In his Word who became incarnate, died, and rose for us, he fills us with his blessings. Through his Word, he pours into our hearts the Gift that contains all gifts, the Holy Spirit. (CCC 1082)

Liturgy as invitation to participate in life of Holy Spirit

It is through the liturgy, and particularly the Eucharist, that God's invitation of love and participation in the life of the Holy Spirit is expressed. God wants to be in relationship with us; that is most clearly shown in the liturgy. The heart of the liturgy is God's invitation to us.

Liturgy as celebrated is invitation.

We can see the invitation dimension of the liturgy in the very way that we celebrate it. Today, we want to look at the three key ways God's invitation is offered to us in our Sunday liturgy.

We experience God's invitation

in the scriptures
in the Eucharist
in the community

- ◆ in the Scriptures
- ◆ in the Eucharist,
- ◆ and in the community.

In the Scriptures

Old Testament reading: God's covenant, commitment, and faithfulness

Each Sunday we hear of the way that God has communicated with people across the ages. In the first reading from the Old Testament, we hear of God's covenant with the Israelites, God's commitment to them as a chosen people. In these readings we hear of God's hope for the Israelites and God's faithfulness toward them—a faithfulness that lasted even when they were not faithful to their covenant with God.

Responsorial psalm expresses a range of responses to God; the psalms provide words we can use to express our own responses.

We respond to that invitation with the responsorial psalm. The psalms are filled with expressions of a wide variety of reactions and feelings about God. Sometimes the psalmist speaks of his great love for God or his confidence in God's presence. In other psalms the psalmist expresses a sense of abandonment and sadness because he feels so alone. In the psalms we find the words to express our own thoughts and feelings to God.

Second reading is from one of the letters on living the Christian life.

The middle reading is from one of the letters written by some of the key leaders in the early Church. We are invited in these readings to recognize the challenge and the promise of living the Christian life, of being a disciple within the community of disciples.

The Gospel reading: stories Jesus told and stories about Jesus

The final reading is the Gospel—an excerpt from Matthew, Mark, Luke, or John. Here we listen to stories about Jesus' life or stories that Jesus told about the Kingdom of God. Jesus, as the living Word of God, speaks God's invitation to us most clearly.

Each of the readings invites us to hear again of God's presence in human history and to grow in our awareness of God's presence in our lives.

Remember that single mom who got up early on Sunday to get reports done for work and spent the rest of the day catching up with things that needed doing around the house? Well, a few Sundays later she went to Mass with her daughters.

(Ask reader representing a working single mom to stand and read from the second Reader Script.)

— 🕊 —

Reader 1: *When I got to Mass today, I felt pretty distracted. I mean, it was hard not to think about the reports I had piled on my desk and the work I could be doing to catch up at home. But as I sat with my daughters I really started listening to the readings. The refrain from Psalm 71 that we sang after the first reading: "Oh, God, Be my rock of refuge, a stronghold to give me safety, for you are my rock and my fortress," was like God was speaking right to me. As a single parent, I really struggle to keep things together at home and at work. When I heard the psalm this morning, I felt like God was inviting me to let him give me the strength I need.*

— 🕊 —

Leader:
Listening to the readings

When we listen—really listen—to the Scriptures as they are proclaimed, we open ourselves up to hear God's invitation. What can we do to encourage this openness? Here are a few suggestions; you can probably think of others.

Arriving in time to get settled

◆ Get to church with enough time to get settled in before the Mass starts. If you are still working with coats or rearranging the kids or reading the bulletin when the Scriptures begin, it is easy to miss the message.

Arriving earlier to read one of the readings

◆ Get to church even earlier to read through the Gospel or one of the other readings. If this seems impossible, find some quiet time on Saturday to look at the readings. Many parishes list the upcoming week's reading in the bulletin. You can also get the Scripture references online; the Web address is in your handout.

Listening rather than reading

◆ Listen to the reading rather than reading along in a missalette. When the readings begin, shift in your seat so you are facing the reader. Be sure to sit in a place where you can both hear and see the reader.

In the Eucharist

Sharing in God's divine life and love

In the Eucharist itself we experience the invitation to share in God's divine life and love. We receive the Body and Blood of Christ under the appearance of bread and wine.

Connection with those around us, with wider community

In receiving the Eucharist, we are connected to those from the past "who have gone before us marked by the sign of faith" (Eucharistic Prayer I). At the same time, we are connected with those present as we move together to receive the Eucharist in Holy Communion. In receiving the Eucharist, we are invited to become more and more aware of our bond with God, with those around us, and in some way with our own deepest selves. We are invited to a time of quiet reflection, but a reflection that moves us toward action.

Remember the young father scrambling to get his kids to soccer practices while balancing work schedules? One Sunday this father and his family did make it to Mass.

(Ask reader representing a busy father to stand and read from the second Reader Script.)

— 🕊 —

Reader 2:   *Between the kids' activities and our work schedules, it can really be tough to get our whole family to Mass on Sunday mornings. But for the past few weeks, my wife and I have just made it a priority to get there. Actually, it's one of the few times we all get in the car and go to the same place. This morning after Communion, the music was playing, and I looked at the boys kneeling there and felt a true sense of peace. After church, we came home and made breakfast together. Going to Mass with the family on Sunday seems to make a difference in our whole day.*

— 🕊 —

Leader: When we enter into the full celebration of liturgy and share in the Eucharist with a fully conscious and active participation, we grow in our awareness of God's invitation to be in union with God and with one another. What can we do to help ourselves grow this awareness? Here are a couple of suggestions; again, you can probably think of others.

Being attentive to the Eucharistic prayer

◆ As in really listening to the Scriptures, attention to the Eucharist requires some focus and discipline. "Zoning out" from time to time during the Eucharistic prayer probably happens to everyone; but when you catch yourself thinking about the myriad of things that you need to do after Mass or should have done before Mass, take a breath, call to mind God's presence, and try to pay careful attention to the words of the Eucharistic prayer.

Fasting as a way to
enhance awareness

◆ We have the obligation to fast for one hour before receiving the Eucharist. But what if we saw the idea of fasting before Eucharist not as obligation but as invitation? We are mindful of the exquisite gift we receive—Jesus Christ present under the appearance of bread and wine. The fasting serves to enhance that awareness.

In the community

We gather as a community.

When we come to Sunday liturgy, we come not simply as an individual or as a part of our family, but we come as members of a faith community. We are a gathering of people who have committed ourselves at some level to live our lives as Christians and as Catholics.

A wide variety of people

It is a diverse group of people that gather each week in this parish and in parishes everywhere. We are spirit-filled, committed Catholics; reluctant teenaged participants; and everyone in between. We come with confidence in God's presence and with the sometimes feeble hope that we are not alone in this vast universe.

Community as a sign
of God's presence

The community of Catholics assembled each Sunday for liturgy is an essential sign of God's presence and invitation to fullness of life. We know the stories of some of them: the young family with active kids involved in lots of activities, the single parent with pressures at work and at home and little time for self, the older couple whose children are grown who remember well their family taking up half a pew and then some, the couple who have exhausted all of the possibilities of having a child together and now must mourn the loss of that dream. All of them—all of us—are gathered by invitation. And it is in this community that we are made more aware of God's presence and invitation.

Think back to the woman who was caring for her parents. The worry and the driving to their home each week was taking up a lot of time and lots of energy. But one Sunday . . .

(Ask reader representing a middle-aged woman to stand and read from the second Reader Script.)

— 🕊 —

Reader 3: *I decided to visit my folks on Saturday so that I could go to Mass on Sunday. One of the intercessions was for people who are dealing with long-term illness. I felt we were praying for my parents. After church, a friend I haven't seen for a while asked how Mom and Dad were doing, and when I told her the struggles they were having, she invited me to lunch during the week. She told me that she found out last year that her dad has Alzheimer's.*

— 🕊 —

Leader: Recognizing the presence and invitation of God in the community is an essential part of being Catholic. How do we grow in our ability to recognize this? Here are a few suggestions.

Greeting people when you come in

- When you arrive for Mass, be sure to greet everyone. We are all coming together for the same reason, so feel free to greet and chat with others who are coming in with you.

Greeting those around you as you sit down

- Our tendency to sit in the same spots each week has some advantages: we do come to recognize the people around us. Greet the ones you recognize; introduce yourself to the ones you don't know. We become a community of faith when we act like a community of faith!

Connecting with others outside liturgy

- Take advantage of every opportunity to connect with others: coffee after Mass, the annual picnic or bazaar *(mention a local parish event here)*. Join with others in this community of faith.

The invitation is there—in Scripture, in Eucharist, and in the community gathered. What would it mean to shift the sense of Sunday Mass from obligation to invitation?

Let's move into some conversation to discuss that.

(Small-group conversation) *(Invite participants to form groups of 6 or 7, including a facilitator. Explain that the groups will have 15 minutes for conversation on the points outlined on the handout.)*

(As the time for small-group conversation comes to a close, invite the participants to bring their attention back to the full group. Invite the small-group facilitators to share insights from their groups.)

REFLECT

(Instrumental music playing softly in the background enhances the sense of prayerfulness.)
(Pause briefly at each / mark.)

As our time together comes to a close, let's take a moment to quiet ourselves and rest in God's presence.

Sit back and get comfortable. Take a deep breath, filling your lungs with air. / If you are comfortable doing so, close your eyes. / Be aware of the rhythm of your own breathing. / As you breathe in, imagine God's love filling your innermost being. / As you breathe out, remember that God's presence surrounds you.

(Allow time for personal reflection.)

Please respond, "We thank you, God!"

> For the invitation to come to your feast.
> (We thank you God!)
> For the gift of gathering with friends.
> (We thank you God!)
> For the opportunity to hear to your Word.
> (We thank you God!)
> For the presence of Jesus in the Eucharist.
> (We thank you God!)

Loving God, we thank you for this time together.
Bless us with the wisdom to make Sunday a special day
   of the week.
Help us make a renewed commitment
   to participate in the Sunday liturgy—
May we enter into our prayer and worship
   with a greater awareness of your love for us,
   and with a deeper appreciation for one another.
Send your Spirit to guide us.
Help us respond to your invitation with open hearts!
We pray this in the name of Jesus, your Son,
Amen.

R E S P O N D

During this time together we've talked about the importance of the Sunday liturgy in our lives. The handout for this session offers creative ways for us to make Sundays and our celebrations of liturgy more meaningful—for us as adults and for our children.

(Refer to the handouts photocopied from pages 124–126.)

"Bringing the Message into Everyday Life" encourages us to make Sunday a day that is different from the rest of the days in the week. Feel free to add your own suggestions to the ones that are listed.

"Bringing the Message Home" shows how God's invitation is present throughout the entire celebration of the Mass. It offers specific ideas about how we can respond to that invitation in our everyday lives. Try choosing one or two of these suggestions to make your family's celebration of the Mass more meaningful.

"Deepening the Message" is a guide to participation in the Sunday liturgy for your personal reflection.

Thank you for taking the time to be here. I hope we will see you back next time *(name the date and time)*, as we continue to examine the question for this year: What does it mean to be Catholic? We'll look at the support and guidance our Catholic faith offers to help us with the moral decisions that face us throughout our lives.

READER SCRIPT
Three Readers Excuse Themselves from Mass

(Leader asks Reader 1 to read.)

Reader 1:
(as a working
single mom)

I am just starting to make some real advances in my job at work. That's important because I'm a single parent, and we depend completely on my salary. On Sunday morning, I get up early while the kids are still sleeping to try to catch up on reports. Then I work on the house, do the laundry, and help the kids with their homework. Before I know it, it's time to go to bed. Sunday is just one more crazy day in the week. Mass? I ask you, consider me excused!

(Leader speaks then asks Reader 2 to read.)

Reader 2:
(as a busy father
of a young family)

I know going to Mass on Sunday is important. I always get something out of it when I go. But it's just so hard to get there. The boys have soccer practice on Sunday morning. Sometimes we travel to games. With both of us working, my wife and I are always scrambling on the weekends to get everything done. When we"re home, sometimes we just sleep in. We're exhausted. Sunday Mass? I ask you, consider me excused!

(Leader speaks then asks Reader 3 to read.)

Reader 3:
(as a middle-aged
woman with
aging parents)

Both of my parents are really starting to show their age. I think my dad is in the beginning stages of Alzheimer's. I worry about them. So every weekend, I go to their house to check on them, make sure there's enough food, and that things are relatively clean. They only live an hour away, but I like to drive there on Sunday mornings when traffic isn't so bad. Go to Mass? Consider me excused!

R E A D E R   S C R I P T
Three Readers Reconsider the Value of Mass

(Leader asks Reader 1 to read.)

Reader 1:
(as a working single mom)

When I got to Mass today, I felt pretty distracted. I mean, it was hard not to think about the reports I had piled on my desk and the work I could be doing to catch up at home. But as I sat with my daughters I really started listening to the readings. The refrain from Psalm 71 that we sang after the first reading: "Oh, God, Be my rock of refuge, a stronghold to give me safety, for you are my rock and my fortress," was like God was speaking right to me. As a single parent, I really struggle to keep things together at home and at work. When I heard the psalm this morning, I felt like God was inviting me to let him give me the strength I need.

(Leader speaks then asks Reader 2 to read.)

Reader 2:
(as a busy father of a young family)

Between the kids' activities and our work schedules, it can really be tough to get our whole family to Mass on Sunday mornings. But for the past few weeks, my wife and I have just made it a priority to get there. Actually, it's one of the few times we all get in the car and go to the same place. This morning after Communion, the music was playing, and I looked at the boys kneeling there and felt a true sense of peace. After church, we came home and made breakfast together. Going to Mass with the family on Sunday seems to make a difference in our whole day.

(Leader speaks then asks Reader 3 to read.)

Reader 3:
(as a middle-aged woman with aging parents)

I decided to visit my folks on Saturday so that I could go to Mass on Sunday. One of the intercessions was for people who are dealing with long-term illness. I felt we were praying for my parents. After church, a friend I haven't seen for a while asked how Mom and Dad were doing, and when I told her the struggles they were having, she invited me to lunch during the week. She told me that she found out last year that her dad has Alzheimer's.

Invitation to the Feast

The documents of the Second Vatican Council remind us that the liturgy is the "summit" toward which the life of the Church is directed and the "font" from which the Church's power flows. But for many people, going to Mass on Sunday is simply an obligation, something to squeeze into a busy weekend or to set aside if the day is too hectic. However, if we consider the liturgy not as an obligation, but rather as an invitation, our perspective might change. The liturgy is an invitation to participate in the life of God. The invitation is present in the words of Scripture, in the gathered assembly, and in the consecrated bread and wine. As we enter into the Sunday liturgy with more attention and care, we can recognize God's invitation and the importance it can have for our lives.

Conversation

The Church earnestly desires that all the faithful should be led to that fully, conscious, and active participation in liturgical celebrations which is demanded by the very nature of the liturgy.

Constitution on the Sacred Liturgy 14

- ◆ Introduce yourself and talk about one insight or new idea you gained from the presentation.

- ◆ What role does the Mass play in your life? Talk about a time when experiencing the Mass was especially meaningful or powerful for you.

- ◆ We can "hear" the invitation to participate in God's life in many ways through the Mass. We talked about three of them in today's session:

  . . . in the Scriptures
  . . . in the Eucharist
  . . . in the community

  Name something you would like to do to make your participation in the Mass more meaningful in one of these areas.

- ◆ Talk about something you already do or would like to do to make Sundays a special day—a day different from the rest—for you and your family.

© Loyola Press

Bringing the Message into Everyday Life

*"For six days you may do your work, but
on the seventh day you must rest."*
Exodus 23:12

We have a long tradition in the Church of keeping the Sabbath holy. But how many of us really make Sunday different from other days in the week, and what does it mean to rest?

Our tradition invites us to rest not necessarily in passive ways, as in resting on the couch, but in more creative ways. On Sunday, we are invited to rest from our usual work, activities, schedules, and routines and take a day to reflect, to be thankful, to listen, to savor and enjoy. Sunday rest is meant to be a time for us to put aside the work of the world so that we have time to recharge our spirits and care for our souls.

Think differently about Sunday. Imagine a day of Sabbath rest . . .

Rest from the usual morning routine. On Sunday . . .
Go to Mass. If you have children, encourage the family to go together. On the way home, ask each person to name something that was special to them—something at Mass they enjoyed.

Rest from driving. On Sunday . . .
Take time to go for a long walk. In your heart, give thanks for the gifts of God's presence around you.

Rest from television. On Sunday . . .
Read a good book or an article you are interested in. Or set aside a special time to read your favorite stories out loud to your children.

Rest from doing your usual work and chores. On Sunday . . .
Take time to sit quietly and reflect on what happened this week. In prayer, name things you are grateful for, things you ask forgiveness for.

Rest from running in different directions, doing errands, and going out. On Sunday . . .
Plan dinner and eat together at the table. Pray before the meal, thanking God for the gifts at the table. Invite everyone to add their own special prayers of petition or thanks.

Rest from trying to do every last thing. On Sunday . . .
Snuggle into bed early. (Remember your prayers!)

© Loyola Press

Bringing the Message Home

Throughout our celebration of the Liturgy, we are invited to respond to God's invitation of love. Here are some ways to help your family respond to this invitation.

Gathering and welcome

God's invitation: All are welcome to share in the feast of Eucharist.

Our response: Look for ways for your family to reach out and welcome others in your parish. Volunteer to serve as greeters. Offer to drive someone to church. Invite a neighbor to come to church with you.

Listening to God's Word

God's invitation: Sunday after Sunday, God speaks to us through the words and stories of the Scriptures.

Our response: Read the Sunday Gospel together as a family before coming to Mass. After Mass, invite family members to talk about their favorite part of the Gospel story— or something from the homily they thought was important. You can find the readings for a particular Sunday at www.nccbuscc.org/nab/index.htm.

Praying for others

God's invitation: During the Eucharist, God invites us to lift up our prayers and concerns in faith.

Our response: Throughout the week, be aware of those in need of prayer. Write these intentions down on slips of paper and place them in a small bowl on your kitchen table. Read over these slips before Mass so that you'll remember to pray for these intentions.

Presenting the gifts

God's invitation: God invites us to bring our gifts to the Eucharistic table.

Our response: Help your child understand that when we offer the bread and wine to God, we also offer the gift of ourselves. Find ways that the children in the parish can participate in the Sunday collection (donating small amounts of money, bringing food for the food pantry, or offering special acts of kindness).

Holy Communion

God's invitation: Eucharist invites us to be nourished by the body and blood of Christ.

Our response: When we receive Jesus in the Eucharist, we are called to be Jesus for one another—to nourish people in need, people who are hungry for care, support, and friendship. After Mass, choose a simple act of service your family will attempt to carry on the work of Christ during the coming week.

Go in peace to love and serve the Lord.

Session D — *Invitation to the Feast*

Handout D3

Deepening the Message

Participating fully in Sunday Liturgy means making room for the liturgy in our lives. The commitment to encourage active participation in the Sunday liturgy is a topic being discussed in many parishes and dioceses across the country. The following excerpts are taken from a 1997 pastoral letter by Cardinal Roger Mahony to the people of the Archdiocese of Los Angeles.

Gather Faithfully Together: A Guide for Sunday Mass
By Cardinal Roger Mahony

"Full" participation brings us to the liturgy, body and soul, with all our might. It begins long before the liturgy in making sure that Sunday Mass is not just one more thing on our "must do" list. (91)

Become people who worship in the midst of the Sunday Liturgy.

Know which Gospel and New Testament letters we are currently reading on Sundays, and use these for daily reading. Bring to the prayer of intercession on Sunday all that you pray for; take from it persons to be remembered daily by you; when you hear the news of the community and the world, hear it as a Christian who must in prayer lift up the world's needs. Mark with prayer your morning rising and your evening going to bed: the Lord's Prayer certainly, but also some song or psalm from the songs and psalms of Sunday Liturgy in your parish. (106)

Become people who prepare themselves for Sunday Liturgy.

Seek little ways that can help you make the Lord's Day as much as possible a day when liturgy has room. Find some habit for Sunday morning that helps you anticipate being together as a Church to do the liturgy. Find just one steady practice that makes you stretch toward the Reign of God we glimpse at Mass: It might be a way to make more real the collection that happens on Sunday for the Church and the poor; extending the peace of Christ that you receive each Sunday to others in need of that peace; or fasting from food or distractions and so becoming thoroughly hungry for God's Word and the Eucharistic banquet. (107)

From Gather Faithfully Together: Guide for Sunday Mass by Cardinal Roger Mahony, Archbishop of Los Angeles Liturgy Training Publications 1997

© Loyola Press

Let Your Conscience Be Your Guide

At the heart of Catholic moral thought are the recognition of the importance of the conscience and the requirement that each person strive to maintain a well-formed conscience. A well-formed conscience serves as a fundamental guide to our making good moral decisions.

If we are to use our consciences effectively, three elements are key: taking time to think about the decision, drawing on the resources of our tradition and of the people around us, and connecting with a community of faith that is shaped by Gospel values. All of these elements, set in a context of prayer, contribute to our ability to make good moral choices and also to the developing maturity of an adult conscience.

Leader's 3-Minute Retreat

As you begin to prepare for this Gathering Session, pause for a moment. Take a few deep breaths and be aware of God's loving presence with you.

Prayerfully read this Old Testament passage from Deuteronomy. Note a phrase or sentence that catches your attention. Just sit with that, perhaps rereading the phrase or sentence a few times.

For Your Reflection

Think about some important decisions you have made in the past. What has helped you to make good moral decisions, to "choose life"?

What decisions are you facing now? Bring these to God in prayer.

> "Here, then, I have today set before you life and prosperity, death and doom. If you obey the commandments of the LORD, your God, which I enjoin on you today, loving him, and walking in his ways, and keeping his commandments, statutes and decrees, you will live and grow numerous, and the LORD, your God, will bless you in the land you are entering to occupy. If, however, you turn away your hearts and will not listen, but are led astray and adore and serve other gods, I tell you now that you will certainly perish; you will not have a long life on the land which you are crossing the Jordan to enter and occupy. I call heaven and earth today to witness against you: I have set before you life and death, the blessing and the curse. Choose life, then, that you and your descendants may live, by loving the LORD, your God, heeding his voice, and holding fast to him."
>
> Deuteronomy 30:15–20

Overview and Agenda

Central Theme

At the heart of Catholic moral thought are the sanctity and integrity of a well-formed conscience.

Objectives

This session is designed to
- provide opportunity for adults to reflect on the role of one's conscience in moral decision making.
- highlight factors that contribute to the development of a well-formed conscience and the resources adult Catholics can use to help make good moral decisions.

Schedule

	Arrival and Greetings
10 minutes	Engage
40 minutes	Explore
20 min	Presentation
20 min	Small-group conversation
10 minutes	Reflect and Respond
	Refreshments

To Do Before the Gathering Session

- [ ] Read the general information on planning and conducting the sessions (page 32).

- [ ] Identify special groups in the parish to invite to this session. These might include Confirmation candidates and their sponsors, parents of children preparing for first Penance, and parish decision makers.

- [ ] Ask a person to read the passages from Deuteronomy during the Engage portion of this session and a person to read the passages from 2 Samuel during the Explore portion of this session. Prepare a Bible with Deuteronomy 30:15–20 and 2 Samuel 11:1–5 clearly marked.

- [ ] Set up a CD player to play instrumental background music during the guided meditation. Time the music to make sure the selection is long enough.

- [ ] Set out handouts for distribution as people arrive.

Background for the Presenter

At the heart of Catholic moral theology is the sanctity of the human conscience. "Their conscience is people's most secret core, and their sanctuary. There they are alone with God whose voice echoes in their depths. By conscience, in a wonderful way, that law is made known which is fulfilled in the love of God and of one's neighbor." (The Church in the Modern World 16) It is this conscience that each person has the right and responsibility to follow (*CCC* 1782).

The writers of the *Catechism of the Catholic Church* recognize the multiple resources that contribute to conscience formation:

God's Word in Scripture, prayer, and the gifts of the Holy Spirit, *"aided by the witness or advice of others and guided by the authoritative teaching of the Church (Cf. DH 14)"*. (1785)

Catholic adults have the responsibility to continually form their conscience in light of Church teaching and human experience. One of the important contributions of adult faith formation is that it provides adults with the opportunity to talk with others about the moral decisions that shape modern life.

Suggested reading
Catechism of the Catholic Church 1776–1802
Christian Morality: In the Breath of God, Russell B. Connors, Jr., Ph.D. Chicago: Loyola Press, 2002.

For the story of David, see 1 Samuel 16–2 Samuel. The story used in Explore can be found in 2 Samuel 11 and 12.

ENGAGE

Focus of session

Welcome, everyone! It is good to come together for this Gathering Session. Thank you for being with us. During this session we will talk about how we make important decisions in our lives. What helps us make good moral decisions—decisions that reflect our values and our faith? What can get in the way of making good moral choices?

All kinds of decisions—some are easier than others

We are constantly faced with making decisions—decisions about family issues, decisions about careers and where we are going to live, decisions about projects we are going to take on, or things we are going to say no to. Some decisions seem fairly easy to make; others can be more difficult.

Decision making—what helped you?

As we begin, I'd invite you to pause for a few moments to think about your own decision making. When you are faced with making an important decision, what kinds of things help you figure out what to do? What steps do you take? Who do you turn to? What do you do?

(Pause for a moment to allow time for reflection.)

Now turn to one or two people sitting next to you. Introduce yourselves. Tell each other how you responded to this question: What helps you make good decisions?

(Allow three or four minutes for conversation.)

Thank you. Keep these thoughts in mind as we listen to a beautiful, yet challenging passage from Deuteronomy.

(A reader comes forward and reads Deuteronomy 30:15–20 from a Bible.)

— 📖 —

Reading:
Deuteronomy 30:15–20

"Here, then, I have today set before you life and prosperity, death and doom. If you obey the commandments of the LORD, your God, which I enjoin on you today, loving him, and walking in his ways, and keeping his commandments, statutes and decrees, you will live and grow numerous, and the LORD, your God, will bless you in the land you are entering to occupy. If, however, you turn away your hearts and will not listen, but are led astray and adore and serve other gods, I tell you now that you will certainly perish; you will not have a long life on the land which you are crossing the Jordan

to enter and occupy. I call heaven and earth today to witness against you: I have set before you life and death, the blessing and the curse. Choose life, then, that you and your descendants may live, by loving the LORD, your God, heeding his voice, and holding fast to him."

The word of the Lord.

— 📖 —

Response: Thanks be to God.

Leader: God,
You have blessed us with the ability to choose.
We may choose to listen to your word.
We may choose not to hear.
We may choose to follow you.
We may choose to turn away.

You are with us during this time together.
Help us become more aware
of your constant loving presence.
Help us listen to your voice inside our hearts.

As we continue to grow in our faith
May the decisions we make
And the direction we choose to take in life
Reflect our love for you and one another.
We pray this in the name of your loving son, Jesus.
Amen.

EXPLORE

Listen again to these words from the Book of Deuteronomy:

Deuteronomy 30:19–20

"I have set before you life and death, the blessing and the curse. Choose life, then, that you and your descendants may live by loving the Lord, Your God, heeding his voice, and holding fast to him."

How do we make good moral choices?

So how do we as adult Catholics go about making the right choices—choosing life over death as the writers of Deuteronomy tell us to do? How do any of us make good moral decisions, decisions that reflect our faith and the values of the Gospel?

How does our conscience come into the discussion?

We started this session by asking you to name what helps you when you are faced with making an important decision. Did any of you name your conscience?

Jiminy Cricket as Pinocchio's conscience

There is a great scene in the movie *Pinocchio,* when Jiminy Cricket is commissioned to be the puppet's conscience. "A conscience?" Pinocchio asks, "What is a conscience?"

"A conscience," Jiminy explains, "is that still, small voice that most people won't listen to."

Place of conscience in Catholic moral thought

Understanding the importance of that still, small voice—conscience—is fundamental in Catholic moral thought. The Constitution on the Church in the Modern World, one of the central documents from the Second Vatican Council, makes this clear. This document describes our conscience as our "most secret core and sanctuary," a place where we are "alone with God." It is in our conscience that we hear God's voice.

Reference to The Constitution on the Church in the Modern World

Our conscience is that "quiet voice" (God's voice) within us, affirming for us what we believe to be true at the deepest part of ourselves. As Catholics, we are called to follow the directives of a "well-formed conscience."

A well-formed conscience

A well-formed conscience isn't something that comes to us automatically. A well-formed conscience is something we need to work at continually throughout our lives.

Guidance from others

Our conscience is formed by all the explicit and implicit directives we received as children and as adults—by all the ways in which we have come to understand what it means to be a good person.

Scripture	In addition, as Catholics we look to the Scriptures for the sense of direction in our lives, for the vision of what a life lived in justice looks like. The Scriptures, as well as the
Church teaching	teachings of the Church, are essential resources for the development of a well-formed conscience.
Community of faith	The Scriptures are given expression for us, lived out for us, through other people and in community. All the people in our lives who have given us examples of what it means to be moral—to act justly—help form our conscience.
Our own experience	Also, our own personal experiences and our reflections on those experiences, as well as the way we have made decisions in the past, influence our conscience in the present.
We are each called to be true to our own conscience.	The result is the unique pattern of personality and moral character that defines each of us as individuals. At the core of this is our conscience—guiding, directing, judging. Clearly, then, our conscience is integral to us, a part of who we are, the core of who we are. It is to our own conscience that we are called to be true.
Using our conscience effectively	It is important for us to remember that a well-formed conscience needs to be listened to when we are called on to make a moral decision. Remember Pinocchio? Even though Jiminy Cricket tried his hardest to keep Pinocchio out of trouble, it often didn't work. Why? Because Pinocchio refused to listen. The same thing can happen to us. Having a well-formed conscience is no guarantee that we'll make good choices.
The example of King David	One of the best examples we have of this is the story of David from the Old Testament. The stories about David that are told in the First and Second Books of Samuel give us an image of one whose relationship with God is strong. At an
background on David	early age David was chosen by God to be the second king of Israel. He fought bravely and vanquished the foes of Israel in the name of the Lord God. Many of the events of David's early life give clear evidence of his faithfulness to God and his ability to make good moral choices.
	And yet, at a crucial point in his life, David didn't attend to his conscience, didn't listen to that "quiet voice" of God.
David's decisions	Let's look at the decisions David made and how he made them so as to draw some insights about what goes into making a good moral decision.
	Once David had become king of Israel and brought some level of peace and unity to the nation, he became more and more powerful. He came to believe that he could do and have anything he wanted because he was favored by God.

Let's hear the account in Second Samuel 11:1–5.

*(A reader comes forward and reads
2 Samuel 11:1–5 from a Bible.)*

— 📖 —

Reading: 2 Samuel 11:1–5

At the turn of the year, when kings go out on campaign, David sent out Joab along with his officers and the army of Israel, and they ravaged the Ammonites and besieged Rabbah. David, however, remained in Jerusalem. One evening David rose from his siesta and strolled about on the roof of the palace. From the roof he saw a woman bathing, who was very beautiful. David had inquiries made about the woman and was told, "She is Bathsheba, daughter of Eliam, and wife of [Joab's armor-bearer] Uriah the Hittite." Then David sent messengers and took her. When she came to him, he had relations with her, at a time when she was just purified after her monthly period. She then returned to her house. But the woman had conceived, and sent the information to David, "I am with child."

— 📖 —

So David saw a woman that he wanted, and even though she was married to someone else, he knew that he had the power to take her, and so he did.

David is in serious moral trouble right off. He sees what he wants and he takes it. The account in Second Samuel gives no indication that David stopped long enough to reflect and to recognize the situation as involving a moral decision.

Without taking time for reflection, David wasn't able to recognize the reasons for his decisions or the consequences that might follow.

Element 1:
Taking time to think about the
decision

So the first element that contributes to making a good, moral decision is taking the time to reflect on the situation, identify the issues, and recognize the options and consequences.

When we don't take time to reflect on our moral decisions, it is easy to miss the variety of options that might be present or the long-term consequences that the various decisions bring with them. Without time for reflection, it is often difficult to name the motivation that is affecting the decision or the values that are involved.

But this reflection isn't done in a vacuum. It is important that we pay attention to the multiple sources that shape our moral context. These include Scripture and Church teaching as well as friends and family.

Element 2:
Drawing on the resources of
our tradition and on the
people around us

So that is the second element of making a good moral decision—drawing on the resources that can bring clarity and insight to our decision making.

Here, too, David set himself up for a bad decision. He failed to attend to the resources that could have helped him with the decision. It is clear in First and Second Samuel that David had a keen sense of God's presence in his life. And what about friends and advisors? Because David didn't draw on the resources that were available to him, his decisions went from bad to worse.

David is informed that Bathsheba is pregnant. Now what is he going to do? First, David does some maneuvering to get Bathsheba's husband, Uriah, to sleep with her. When that doesn't work, David orders the commander of his armies to put Uriah in a dangerous setting and then pull back so that he is killed in battle. Basically, David had Uriah killed in order to cover up his first bad decision.

What is clear in this account of the story is that David saw himself as being above everyone else, above the community of Israelites. He made his decisions without reference to the community that he served as king. Since he was king, David thought that he could do anything he wanted. He failed to recognize that his decisions would have ramifications for all of Israel.

Element 3:
Connecting with a community
of faith that is shaped
by Gospel values

This is the third element: it is essential that moral decisions are situated within the context of a faith community. It is in the community of faith that we find the support that enhances our ability to attend to that inner voice.

The faith community—our local parish—can serve as a safe environment where contemporary moral issues can be discussed with openness and in the context of faith. Staying connected with the community serves to remind us that we aren't alone in making these moral decisions. In fact, we have the models of the saints across history who have struggled to respond faithfully to the moral challenges of their own day.

We have looked at three key elements that contribute to a good moral decision: taking time for reflection, drawing on available resources, and staying connected with the community of faith.

The context of prayer

And one more thing—not another element but the context within which all elements make sense: we make moral decisions in the context of prayer.

A fundamental conviction permeating Catholic thought is that our relationship with God is marked by gracious invitation. God is always inviting us into a relationship of love, a relationship that calls us to respond in faith. As we struggle to make moral decisions—and some of these decisions are very difficult—we do so knowing that God is with us, inviting us to see signs of his presence all around us.

Reflection, resources, and community, all in the context of prayer—how are these elements present in your own moral decision making? Let's explore this question in conversation.

(Small-group conversation)

(Invite participants to form groups of 6 or 7, including a facilitator. Explain that the groups will have 15 minutes for conversation on the points outlined on the handout.)

(As the time for small-group conversation comes to a close, invite the participants to bring their attention back to the full group. Invite the small-group facilitators to share insights from their groups.)

REFLECT

(Instrumental music playing softly in the background enhances the sense of prayerfulness.)

(If the children in the parish are using the Finding God series, tell the participants that the children often experience guided meditation as part of their prayer.)

As this Gathering Session comes to a close, let's take time to pray and ask God to guide us with decisions we face in our own lives right now.

One of the most beautiful ways to pray is with guided meditation. Guided meditation invites us to pray with our imaginations. Children are especially good at this. Adults can be, too, if we let ourselves be open!

During this guided meditation we are going to imagine what it would be like to meet Jesus face to face. We talk with Jesus about our lives—about a decision we are trying to make. We listen to Jesus as he talks with us.

(Pause briefly at each / mark.)

We begin by quieting ourselves and becoming aware of God's presence.

Make yourself comfortable. / Relax your muscles. / Gather any tension in your body and let it slowly flow out of you. / The tension in your neck, let it slip away. / The tension in your shoulders, feel it leave. / The tension in your arms and legs, release it. /

Feel all tension drifting away. / Let go of your worries, distractions, concerns, and tiredness. / If you are comfortable doing so, close your eyes. Listen to the sound of your own breathing as you inhale and exhale, inhale and exhale. / Open your mind and heart to God and listen. /

Imagine that you see a door. You walk up to the door and open it.

Outside you see a beautiful lake. Sunlight is glistening off the blue water. There is no one in sight. Step outside and walk toward the lake.

Take a deep breath. The air is fresh and sweet. Birds are flying overhead. Waves are gently lapping the shore. Bend down and take off your shoes. Walk down the sandy beach to the water. The water feels cool on your bare feet.

As you walk along the beach, you see a man standing up ahead. He turns to you, smiles, and waves.

As you get closer, the man looks at you as if he knows you. He greets you by name.

You know now that this man is Jesus.

He is glad to see you and asks if it's all right to join you.

The two of you walk by the water. The sunlight feels warm on your face. A cool breeze blows softly off the water. For a while you walk quietly together. Then Jesus turns to you. He wonders how you're doing.

Take time to tell Jesus. Tell him about the kind of day you've had or about what's going on in your life.

(Pause.)

As you talk, you can tell that Jesus is really interested.

Maybe there's a decision you are trying to make right now— something you've been thinking about for a while, something you're trying to figure out. Maybe it's a decision about work or about your family. Maybe there's a situation you're worried about. You're just not sure what to do.

Now is a good time to talk to Jesus about this decision or about anything else that may be worrying you.

As you talk, you can tell that Jesus is listening, really listening.

(Pause.)

When you are finished talking, Jesus tells you he understands. Then he asks a few questions. Perhaps he asks if there is someone you can talk this over with.

Or he might ask if you have taken time to pray about this decision.

After you answer, Jesus looks at you and assures you of his love. He tells you he is always there to listen and to help.

Jesus asks if there is anything you need from him right now.

Tell Jesus what you need.

(Pause.)

Before you go, Jesus invites you to pray with him and ask the Holy Spirit to guide you.

With an open heart, take this time to pray with Jesus.

Together, you ask the Holy Spirit to help you.

(Pause.)

It's time to go. As you start to walk back, look at Jesus and thank him for this time together.

Tell him you'll be back.

Jesus smiles and tells you to come to him as often as you like.

Jesus stops and waves as you keep walking.

Slowly, you leave the lake and walk back toward the door.

Open the door and gradually bring yourself back to this room, back to all of us gathered here.

When you are ready, open your eyes.

(Pause.)

Welcome back.

RESPOND

Thank you for being open to praying with guided mediation.

During this time together we've talked about the way we as adult Catholics make decisions in our lives. By taking time for reflection, by drawing on the resources of the Church and of our friends and family, and by making the decision in the context of a faith community, we will make better decisions than we would on our own. The handouts for this session offer additional suggestions for helping us make good decisions.

(Refer to the handouts photocopied from pages 141–143.)

"Bringing the Message into Everyday Life" invites you to work through a decision you are facing with a practical (and faithful) step-by-step process.

"Bringing the Message Home" offers a mini-retreat for families. The retreat takes place within the setting of a family meal and provides a creative way for you to talk with your children about the way our faith and values can help us with decisions we face every day.

"Deepening the Message" is an excerpt from an article by Jim Dinn on the development and exercise of conscience.

Thank you for taking the time to be here. I hope you found our gathering to be valuable. God bless you!

Let Your Conscience Be Your Guide

At the heart of Catholic moral thought are the recognition of the importance of the conscience and the requirement that each person strive to maintain a well-formed conscience. A well-formed conscience serves as a fundamental guide to our making good moral decisions.

In order to use our consciences effectively three elements are key: taking time to think about the decision, drawing on the resources of our tradition and of the people around us, and connecting with a community of faith that is shaped by Gospel values. All of these elements, set in a context of prayer, contribute to our ability to make good moral choices and also to the developing maturity of an adult conscience.

Conversation

> Their conscience is people's most secret core and sanctuary. There they are alone with God, whose voice echoes in their depths. By conscience, in a wonderful way, that law is made known which is fulfilled by love of God and of one's neighbor.
>
> The Church in the Modern World 16

- Introduce yourself and talk about one insight or new idea you gained from the presentation.

- In the presentation, three key elements were named as important to making good moral choice:

  . . . taking time to think about the decision

  . . . drawing on the resources of our tradition and of the people around us

  . . . connecting with a community of faith that is shaped by Gospel values

  Talk about a time when you were faced with making an important decision. Which of these elements helped you make this decision? Which of these did you neglect or bypass?

- Think about your own moral foundation. What contributed most to your development of a well-formed conscience? What are some ways that each of us can enhance the conscience formation of the young people in our parish?

Bringing the Message into Everyday Life

Taking steps to make a good decision

Some decisions are easy to make and have little consequence, such as what to fix for dinner or what to wear to work. Other decisions are much more important and can be harder to make. These are decisions that will shape the contours of our lives and set the path for later decisions. Here are simple, yet effective, steps you can use when you are faced with making an important decision. Make an effort to use these steps to work through decisions you are facing right now.

- Think about a significant decision you are facing in your life right now: about work, about your family, about making a change in your life, about finances.

- Write down the situation and the decision you face. Then take time to go through the following steps to help you make your decision. As you begin each of these three steps, take time for prayer, asking God for guidance.

Step 1. Take time to think about the decision.

In a way that is helpful for you, name the options that are involved. Then list the "pros" and "cons," the positive consequences and the negative consequences of choices you could make. You might do this while taking a quiet walk in a peaceful setting, sitting down with pad and pen and listing the options and naming the benefits and losses, or writing in a journal about the conflicts you are feeling about the decision.

Step 2. Draw on the resources of our tradition and on the people around you.

Name people you know whose opinion you respect and whose lives are marked by a sense of justice and charity. Talk with some of these people about the decision you face. Remember, this isn't an opinion poll where the decision with the highest score wins; you are trying to identify the best options and the possible consequences in order to make your *own* decision.

Looking at the resources of our Catholic Tradition can sometimes seem overwhelming. However, talking with people who are well acquainted with Church teaching—your pastor, a director of religious education, or a spiritual director, for example—is a good place to start.

Step 3. Stay connected with a community of faith that is shaped by Gospel values.

Staying connected with the faith community reminds us that we aren't alone. Remember that there are probably others in your parish who have faced a similar moral issue.

Bringing the Message Home

One of the best ways for parents to help children learn about making good moral choices is to practice making real-life decisions together. Here is a simple suggestion for a mini-retreat for you and your family to enjoy—a time for you to talk about your faith and values, and to practice making good decisions about situations that face all of us in everyday life. Read over the retreat; adapt it to fit your style. And then take time to do it.

Preparation

In advance, write out questions that ask your children to make a decision about a real-life situation, each on a separate piece of paper. Use the questions below to give you ideas and add some of your own. Place the questions in a bowl on the table.

1. A grocery store clerk gives you more change than he should. Do you tell him and give the money back, or do you keep the extra money?

2. You are spending the night with a friend who wants to go to a movie that you know your parents do not want you to see. What would you do?

3. A friend at school tells you that he stayed up late last night watching television and didn't get his homework done. He asks to copy yours. What do you tell your friend?

4. You are going down a steep hill on a skateboard. You start to fall, so you jump off. You are fine, but the skateboard crashes into your neighbor's car parked on the side of the road. The skateboard puts a scratch and a small dent on the car door. No one is around. What would you do? Would you tell your neighbor or just leave?

Mealtime retreat

Select a time when your family can sit down together for a meal. Before you eat, light a candle on the table, take the phone off the hook, and begin with a prayer of grace, asking God to bless the food and your time together.

During the meal, invite each person to take a slip of paper out of the bowl and respond to the question. Then discuss the situation with one another. These additional questions might help to keep the conversation going.

◆ What would you be tempted to do?

◆ What do you hope you would do?

◆ What would help you make a good decision?

◆ What does your faith tell you? What do your values tell you?

End with this simple prayer of thanks:

Loving God,
Thank you for the gift of our family.
Help us encourage one another to make good decisions every day.
May our actions show those around us that we believe in you. Amen.

Deepening the Message

Should we let our conscience be our guide?
By Jim Dinn

The Second Vatican Council describes conscience as an intimate personal encounter with God, as "people's most secret core and their sanctuary. There they are alone with God whose voice echoes in their depths" (*Gaudium et Spes,* The Church in the Modern World). It is an awesome perspective, personalizing the exercise of conscience and implicitly linking moral choices with final judgment by reminding us that God collaborates in the very decisions for which he will judge us.

The conscience of even the most enlightened and principled person is always evolving because the formation of conscience is a lifelong process. Childhood faith formation cannot suffice to guide a lifetime of adult moral judgments. Religious education, reflection on scripture, prayer, experience, the advice and example of others, gifts of the Holy Spirit, virtuous habits, and attention to the authoritative teachings of the church— these are among the formative influences on our conscience

But an adult conscience is not achieved by passive, uncritical absorption of authoritative precepts. It develops from a dynamic process, which the U.S. bishops describe in their pastoral letter *Our Hearts Were Burning Within Us:* "Adults need to question, probe, and critically reflect on the meaning of God's revelation in their unique lives in order to grow closer to God."

Catholics sometimes sense an ambiguity in the church's support for individual conscience. On the one hand, the church, as a responsible mother, advocates her children's development into maturity and autonomy. At the same time, like many a protective parent, the church sometimes tries to spare her offspring from bad choices by making decisions for them.

Attending to the development and exercise of our conscience is a key to our liberation and personal integration. The *Catechism of the Catholic Church* notes, "The education of the conscience guarantees freedom and engenders peace of heart."

from "Glad You Asked: Q&A on Church Teaching"
U.S. Catholic, February 2002

Acknowledgments

Excerpts from "Principles of Dialogue" from *Called to Be Catholic* taken with permission from Common Ground Initiative, The National Pastoral Life Center, New York, NY. www.nplc.org.

Excerpts from *Catechism of the Catholic Church*. English translation of the *Catechism of the Catholic Church* for the United States of America copyright © 1994, United States Catholic Conference, Inc.—Libreria Editrice Vaticana.

Excerpts from "Gather Faithfully Together: A Guide for Sunday Mass" by Cardinal Roger Mahony, Archbishop of Los Angeles copyright © 1997 used with permission from the Archdiocese of Los Angeles.

Excerpts from the *General Directory for Catechesis* © 1997 Libreria Editrice Vaticana-United States Conference of Catholic Bishops, Inc., Washington, DC. All rights reserved.

Excerpts from the *New American Bible* with Revised New Testament and Psalms Copyright © 1991, 1986, 1970 Confraternity of Christian Doctrine, Inc., Washington, DC. All rights reserved. No portion of the *New American Bible* may be reprinted without permission in writing from the copyright holder.

Excerpts from *Our Hearts Were Burning Within Us: A Pastoral Plan for Adult Faith Formation in the United States* copyright © 1999 United States Conference of Catholic Bishops, Inc., Washington, DC. No portion of this text may be reproduced by any means without permission from the copyright holder.

"Prayer for a Questioning Heart" from *Seasons of Your Heart* copyright © 1991 by Macrina Wiederkehr, O.S.B. HarperCollins Publishers, Inc.

Excerpts from "Catch the Dream" by Father Charles Faso and "May the Circle Be Unbroken: Why Catholics Treasure Their Saints" by Sister Elizabeth Johnson, C.S.J. and Kathy Coffey copyright © 1994 *U.S. Catholic*. Reproduced by permission from the October and November 1994 issues of *U.S. Catholic*. Subscriptions: $22/year from 205 West Monroe, Chicago, IL 60606; Call 1-800-328-6515 for subscription information or visit http://www.uscatholic.org.

Excerpts from "Should we let our conscience be our guide?" by Jim Dinn in the February 2002 edition of "Glad You Asked: Q&A on Church Teaching" copyright © 2002 *U.S. Catholic*. Reproduced from the February 2002 issue of *U.S. Catholic*. Subscriptions: $22/year from 205 West Monroe, Chicago, IL 60606; Call 1-800-328-6515 for subscription information or visit http://www.uscatholic.org.

Excerpts from Vatican conciliar, postconciliar, and papal documents are from the official translations. Libreria Editrice Vaticana, 00120 Citta del Vaticano.